PRAISE FOR INFLUENCER

Adam Houlahan has written another smart, timely and hugely practical book. *Influencer* is going to help anyone who is struggling to be heard amongst the enormous amount of clutter that we all face. A gem that I read in one sitting and one that I will certainly pick up time and time again.

— Andrew Griffiths, international bestselling author, global entrepreneurial speaker
www.linkedin.com/in/griffithsandrew
www.andrewgriffiths.com.au

You know how it is — you see a 'how to' book and even before you open it you know it's going to be full of phrases like 'I did this', 'my experience is….' and so on. The book becomes all about them and their story. Adam Houlahan doesn't fall into that trap. He's way too humble for that. This is what I call a 'YOU' book. It is literally all about YOU. And it's all about doing the right thing and doing it purposefully so you feel great about doing what Adam gently suggests you should do. The 9 Steps are brilliant. Follow them … you'll become a much more powerful, purposeful you. And you'll leave (and live) a great legacy as a direct result.

— Paul Dunn, 4x Tedx Speaker, Chairman of The Global Giving
Movement B1G1
www.linkedin.com/in/paulb1g1
www.B1G1.com

I binge-read this book. I didn't intend to, but once I started I had to keep going. I have read so many posts, books, etc, that have 'the magic formula' for social-media success. Adam does not promise this, despite his clear success as a LinkedIn influencer. He makes it perfectly clear that LinkedIn is a long-term game. There is stuff in this book about LinkedIn that I had never heard of, even though I have been using the platform for some years. That, plus the nine accelerators that Adam describes, make this the most valuable social-media book I have encountered. I especially appreciated the 'content mix' strategy. I have been a follower of Adam for five years now. Social media in general, and LinkedIn in particular, have changed a lot over that time, but there are still gurus out there peddling the same old stuff. Stick with Adam's advice and you know you will be at the front of the pack in the latest trends.

— Bronwyn Reid, author of *Small Company, Big Business*
  https://www.linkedin.com/in/bronwynreid
  www.bronwynreid.com.au

There's a growing movement towards responsible leadership with a purpose. Making a difference to the lives of others through sharing what you know or what you've learned is a mission being accepted by more and more leaders around the world. It's not about becoming famous, or being known, it's about becoming a positive role model and influencer. And if you want to influence others positively you must read this book on how to do it right. Adam Houlahan is a positive leader in helping *others* become positive leaders.

— Hunter Leonard, author of *Generation Experience*, marketing strategist, speaker and philanthropist
  www.linkedin.com/in/hunter-leonard
  www.silverandwise.com.au

Adam delivers once again with *Influencer*. This nine-step guide will help anyone become a LinkedIn expert, create influence and trust, and build relationships with potential clients. The steps are clearly articulated, easy to follow, and filled with nuggets of truth. Once pointed out, some of the content made me slap my forehead with how obvious they were yet I have never implemented them well. Thank you, Adam; this book will be the bible for LinkedIn that I will go back to read again and again.

— Clare Sheng, author of *The Suit Book: Everything You Need to Know About Wearing a Suit*

www.linkedin.com/in/clare-sheng

www.thefittingroomonedward.com

LinkedIn is an elusive beast; for years I'd tried to tame it and make it my friend. But no matter how long I toiled over creating the perfect post to go with the perfect picture or the perfect video, the beast constantly eluded me. Adam's new book, *Influencer*, shares advanced strategies for building trust and credibility that are essential reading. For me, finding the bolder, more expansive purpose of my business has been priceless. My ultimate goal is to be placed in the 0.02 percent of people on LinkedIn: to be an influencer. And as Adam often states in his book, 'You will only achieve influencer status when other people say you have, not when *you* do.'

— Victoria Rose, author of *How to Make the Rest of Your Life the Best of Your Life*

www.linkedin.com/in/victoriaroseleadership

www.TheLeadershipVoice.com

Social media has created a massive sea of sameness with many professionals struggling to stand out and attract the level of clients they deserve. Adam has prepared a step-by-step process to be able to position yourself as a person of influence on what I would call the world's most powerful business platform. The double bonus with this book is that it is straightforward and easy to understand; however, the strategies are simple to implement and deliver results. It is a book that should not be read and put down. You should keep it on hand and treat it as a manual to refer to so you can continually increase your influence.

— Steve Brossman, author of *Stand Up, Stand out or Stand Aside*
    www.linkedin.com/in/stevebrossman
    https://stevebrossman.com

I have been a LinkedIn user for more than ten years, and thought I had a pretty good network and was visible to both recruiters and business prospects. About six months ago I was lucky enough to read Adam Houlahan's book, *The LinkedIn Playbook*, and realised that I had absolutely no idea of what I didn't know about the power of LinkedIn, and how to optimise my profile to be visible and to build a genuine network of valued contacts.

In his new book, *Influencer*, Adam takes using LinkedIn to the next level and shows you concisely how to become a true influencer in your industry or niche by being known, liked and trusted. Adam also presents compelling case studies to demonstrate how, by applying the nine accelerators of influence, you can quickly elevate your influence and accelerate your business growth. This book is a must-read for anyone who uses LinkedIn.

— Michael Williams, author of *Power Profits: A Comprehensive 9-Step Framework for Reducing Electricity Costs and Boosting Profits*
    www.linkedin.com/in/michael-williams-altusenergy
    http://altusenergy.com.au

If you're looking to grow your influence in your field, look no further than *Influencer*; Adam Houlahan shares his secrets of influencer success. In this practical, no-nonsense book, you will learn the fundamentals required to build your profile, craft your message and resonate powerfully with your ideal client. Known for his LinkedIn training expertise, Adam includes practical advice on how to maximise and leverage your LinkedIn profile. He takes it many steps further, challenging you to assess your website and other digital platforms, as well as explaining how to craft your pitch so your ideal clients know exactly what you're talking about, and ultimately selling to them. This is a must-read book for anyone looking to improve their business, grow their profile and make an impact in their community.

— Rebecca Coomes, author of the world's first SIBO cookbooks, host of *The Healthy Gut* podcast

www.linkedin.com/in/rebeccacoomes

www.thehealthygut.com

One thing I love about Adam Houlahan is his ability to provide extreme value in the most logical and practical way. His previous two books, now well worn, have been my go-to guides to building an online profile, especially on LinkedIn, and now *Influencer* will join them. If you want to become influential in your industry then this book is a must-read. It's the perfect companion to *The LinkedIn Playbook* or for use as a stand-alone resource.

— Katie Marshall, author of *Chicks and Mortar: A Woman's Guide to Investing in Property*

www.linkedin.com/in/katiemarshallau

www.chicksandmortar.com.au

Adam Houlahan's new book, *Influencer*, is another must-have. Concise, easy to read and even easier to understand and implement, this short, sharp book is definitely a best-in-class effort from a guy who knows the ins and outs of using LinkedIn ethically to grow your business, personal brand and influence. The three pillars and nine steps break down Adam's know-how into easy-to-follow, logical steps that build upon each other to deliver influencer status. (But let's be clear, you have to do the work; the book makes it easier to become an influencer, but you have to implement the steps.)

While a standalone in its own right, it is also the perfect companion to his previous book, *The LinkedIn Playbook*. Adding the two together just about guarantees that LinkedIn will become a source of near effortless sales and influence in your chosen marketplace.

Highly recommended. This book will be on my desk alongside Adam's other two books as must-haves: on hand, ready references for ensuring that LinkedIn becomes a business tool that produces the results I am looking for.

— Geoff Hetherington, The Clarity CEO

www.linkedin.com/in/geoffhetherington

www.elitebusinessinstitute.com

www.theclarityceo.com

I thought *The LinkedIn Playbook* was fantastic and got some great wins from the strategies. After finishing *Influencer*, I was blown away. The techniques and concepts are clearly laid out, and it is as simple as doing what Adam says. I can't wait to implement the advice.

— Emily Chatham

www.linkedin.com/in/emily-chatham

Adam Houlahan's *Influencer* is the real-life practical manual on how to use LinkedIn like a pro. The strategies are easy to understand and straightforward to implement. Adam explains his nine-step process in a manner that is very relatable, and sure to empower you to become a true influencer in your industry. More importantly, you'll build a marketing tool that helps you to build a tribe of your potential clients. *Influencer* is a must-read for anyone planning to have a presence on LinkedIn. Adam knows his stuff.

— Robert James, author of Amazon bestseller *Balance: How to Make Your Business and Family Life Work Together*
https://www.linkedin.com/in/robert-james-1b44b6ab
https://balance.enterprises

It's not often that someone delivers a book that's both enjoyable to read and filled with pragmatic advice. Adam has achieved that with *Influencer*; I started implementing his recommendations before I'd finished reading the book.

— Paul Henderson, author of *The Chief Capability Officer* and *The Outcome Generation*
https://www.linkedin.com/in/qualitycvs
www.qualitycvs.co.uk

I have just finished reading Adam Houlahan's book, *Influencer: The 9-Step Guide to Becoming Highly Influential in Any Industry.* Boy, was it an eye-opener! After posting daily on LinkedIn for the last six months, I did not get the traction I had hoped for. I now understand why, and what I need to do to get prospective clients to know me, like me and trust me so they will buy. Thank you, Adam,

for turning the daunting task of navigating LinkedIn into simple and doable steps that l can manage. I will be recommending this book to all my clients.
— Andrea Felton, author of *Organise & Thrive*
  www.linkedin.com/in/andrea-felton
  www.andreafelton.com

Adam Houlahan is the LinkedIn guru; his wealth of knowledge and generosity makes being a part of his community a pleasure. Once again he nails it with *Influencer*, which is a practical, step-by-step guide for anyone looking to be seen as an influencer in their industry.
— Ann Wilson
  https://www.linkedin.com/in/annwilson4
  www.independentink.com.au

I would highly recommend *Influencer*, by Adam Houlahan, to anybody wanting to elevate their professional profile. The book combines step-by-step instructions with tips and research, and is crystal clear on how to start or to enhance your profile on LinkedIn. There are case studies, examples and even scripts throughout the book. Adam has included everything you need. *Influencer* is perfect for somebody starting out, all the way through to people trying to take their profile to the next level. I highly recommend that anybody who wants to elevate their professional status reads this book.
— Carolyn S Dean, author of *Fully Booked: Dental Marketing Secrets for a Full Appointment Book*
  https://www.linkedin.com/in/carolyndean
  https://fullybookeddentist.com

Influencer is the game-changing book every information-hungry-yet-time-poor entrepreneur needs to read. With every chapter comes another penny-dropping moment. Whilst I've had a vague awareness of how I should be using LinkedIn, I wasn't aware of the simple yet highly effective things I could be doing right now today to explode its potential.

Adam's latest book is on point with relevant easy-to-follow steps on how to maximise what I now know to be one of the most powerful tools I can use to share, educate and inspire. If you're in business and serious about being heard in your industry, then *Influencer* by Adam Houlahan is a must-read.
— Natalie Stevens, author of Amazon #1 bestseller *Building Home*
    https://www.linkedin.com/in/natstevens16
    https://buildinoz.com.au

No matter what you are trying to achieve, it's always good to have a methodology to keep you heading in the right direction when you veer off course. This is exactly what *Influencer* by Adam Houlahan is. If you want to know how to become more influential in order to make a bigger impact in your industry, then this book is the blueprint on how to do so.
— Tracy Angwin, Australian Payroll Association
    https://www.linkedin.com/in/tracyangwin
    www.austpayroll.com.au

Influencer is an easy-to-follow, step-by-step guide to building your profile through LinkedIn. If you want to be in the top percentage of people creating impact and able to stand out in a crowded market space then this book is a must-read. Before I read this book, I had a LinkedIn profile but was very linked out. Having read and implemented the practical steps in Adam's book, I now consider myself properly LinkedIn.

— Melissa McConaghy, author of *The New Parkinson's Treatment: Exercise is Medicine*
https://www.linkedin.com/in/melissa-mcconaghy-2b9212
www.pdwarrior.com

Before I read Adam Houlahan's *Influencer*, I was a LinkedIn novice. The owner of a bricks-and-mortar business and author of a bestselling book, I had assumed that LinkedIn was best suited to the B2B sector and would never work for me. How wrong I was. In his excellent book, Adam has not only convinced me that I need LinkedIn in my life, he's cracked a vital marketing code that once had me so confused. Full of practical, personal and proven tips, it shares a simple strategy for success that just makes sense, even to rookies like me.

— Sonja Walker, author of bestseller *School Ready: A Practical and Supportive Guide for Parents With Sensitive Kids*
https://www.linkedin.com/in/sonja-walker-90a89b12
www.kids-first.com.au

INFLUENCER

THE 9-STEP GUIDE
TO BECOMING
HIGHLY INFLUENTIAL
IN ANY INDUSTRY

ADAM HOULAHAN

Author of Amazon bestsellers *Social Media Secret Sauce* and *The LinkedIn Playbook*

Published by Stenica Pty Ltd 2018

A catalogue record for this book is available from the National Library of Australia.

Book cover design and formatting services by BookCoverCafe.com

www.adamhoulahan.com

ISBN: 978-0-9924698-4-9 (pbk)

This book is dedicated to one of my longest serving mentors and business advisors, my good mate, Raymond P Wood. As an author and speaker, you'd think words would come easily to me. They fail me right now in expressing my love and respect for this pillar of the human race, beyond my heartfelt gratitude to him for the positive influence he has been. Without his guidance and, most importantly, friendship I would not be at this point in my life.

Thank you, you bloody legend!

CONTENTS

FOREWORD

Have you noticed it, too? Because it seems to me that most codes of law, ethical principles, spiritual texts, and certainly the Bible all encourage, declare, or command the influence of self and of others. And this may be through personal transformation, mindset shifts, living by example, being an authority, growing followership, increasing discipline, making disciples, and restoring and developing relationships. Have you noticed that personal and societal development, and progress are all governed by a process of influence?

If you think about the purpose of life, it isn't to work, it isn't to have fun, and it isn't even to procreate (some people can't, so that means it can't be the purpose of all lives). The purpose of life is to influence.

In particular, it is to influence yourself and others to motivate positive change. The change may be some sort of personal or business growth. The change may be in the work that you do. Or that change may be from a state of not having fun to one that's far more enjoyable. You might even be influencing someone to change from whatever they are doing and to commence activities that are a prerequisite for procreation.

And with at least three bestselling books, at least four years of friendship with me, and at least five children, Adam Houlahan knows how to influence, whether that's through the vehicles of work, having fun or procreation. :)

Yes, Adam is a master of influence. Not manipulation, but authentic, real, trustworthy leadership that people want to follow and learn from. I've seen it firsthand in his interviews I listened to over six years ago, the keynotes I've seen him deliver in different parts of the world, and his mastermind sessions I've attended. Oh, and in his webinars, live-feedback sessions, posts, programs, courses and books, Adam Houlahan shares no-nonsense, practical and relevant ideas that will increase the breadth and depth of your influence in a fast-changing world. And his ideas work.

I've also seen him directly influence me to grow my influence and my business using the strategies and methodologies he shares, and I've seen him indirectly influence me to increase the ways I've made a positive giving difference in the world by the way he lives his values through his global giving (the work he does has created well over a million impacts in global projects helping the poor and disadvantaged).

I already know that Adam influences thousands upon thousands of people to do the same. It's one thing to influence, but it's quite another to teach others to do it also, and with authenticity and care. He teaches you and me to become even more influential by his creation of structured and implementable processes that generate and increase value. His proven processes make sense, and you and I can replicate them. And he cares that we do.

I think that's awesome. Because when you become more influential, you can influence more people to take positive action, which means you can motivate even more positive change, and since that is the purpose of life, Adam has actually written a book that helps you achieve your life's purpose, and that's exciting ... *if* you implement.

Like faith, purpose without action is dead.

So, read on, apply what you learn, and have faith that you will influence yourself and others to even greater levels of positive change, on purpose.

Have you noticed that everything you have, believe and do, and who you are—your life—has been shaped and influenced? Yesterday influenced your today. Today you can influence your tomorrow. Now ...

... it's your turn. Yes, you can.

Tim Wade
Global conference speaker on motivation and change
www.timwade.com

INTRODUCTION

Influence: The ability to be a compelling force or to produce effects on the actions, behaviour, opinions of others.

Like it or not, we live in a digital world, where instant fame and its financial rewards can be just one viral post away. We hear stories almost daily of people becoming overnight millionaires simply by winning a lottery of some description, yet few of us personally know anyone who has achieved such overnight good fortune.

Equally, we could search online right now and find examples of people who have had the good fortune to capture on camera at the right time their pets, children or friends doing something a little out of the ordinary, funny, or dangerous that the online global community has found worthy of interaction, and the content has gone viral.

This is the influence of our social platforms at work. Instant (though usually fleeting) fame and financial rewards have been achieved with seemingly little or no effort. Yet like those lottery winners very few of us personally know any of these overnight 'instafamous' people.

To some degree, influence can also be gained by having a healthy bank account, or a position of authority. These versions of influence can be maintained with little or no respect for the individual. We might be envious of the wealth or status of these people, but more than likely we speak of them in negative vernacular at every opportunity.

Let me share with you what this book is *not* about.

If you're looking for the secrets to creating overnight fame and fortune, you won't find them here. This book is not about online hacks, and it does not contain tips on viral posts to promote on various social platforms, leading to instant stardom and wealth. Equally, you'll find nothing about gaining a position above others enabling you to force your will upon them, or about buying agreement for your opinions or desires.

This book is written for those who choose to use their knowledge and expertise as forces for good, and by doing so earn the respect of their peers, and those they have the privilege to serve and impact in profound ways.

It's for those who wish to affect change in a positive manner, through self-improvement, which means they deliver their value to the world with a sense of commitment and purpose.

If this sounds like you then read on. You will discover that there are three key requirements, or pillars, that create the recipe for (and the hitherto secret ingredients of) influence:

1. Getting known
2. Being liked
3. Being trusted

Each of these three pillars has three accelerators. Understanding the role of these three pillars, and the accompanying three accelerators, is the key to creating your action plan so that you can also appear to become an overnight success. I will begin by identifying the nine accelerators and explaining why they matter.

1. **Your online profile.** Your profile is your greatest asset, yet it is fragile. Years of building a credible presence can be destroyed overnight. We'll cover the process for creating and protecting yours for years to come.

2. **Microniches.** When you attempt to appeal to everyone you attract no one; in today's hyper-competitive environment it's essential to dominate a *microniche*. We dive deeply into this concept and look at how you can discover yours, and why this accelerator could change the way you market yourself forevermore.

3. **Message.** Clarity around the value you deliver and what it is you stand for is paramount in creating influence. I'll share with you a simple framework to use to get very clear about who you are, what you do and whom you do it for.

4. **Stories.** We're in a story-telling age, and the most important story of all is yours, closely followed by that of your clients, and the product or service you deliver. How you tell these stories is critical to becoming influential.

5. **Engagement.** While the world is focused on the metrics of people who engage with our content, true influencers measure their own engagement in a very different way. I will share with you the process of measuring yours and understanding why.

6. **The power of content.** There are five types of content to focus on, and the mix is important. Of the nine accelerators, the content you create and whom you create it for will create your pathway to success.

7. **Community.** Influencers polarise their audience and embrace the people who believe what they believe. It's not your task to change the opinion of anyone who has one and chooses to express it; your role is to find your tribe and nurture it in order to deliver your greatest value to those willing to accept it.

8. **Problem solving.** When problems are solved, you swim in rivers of gold. The majority of people online are there to be entertained, or to find a solution to a problem; once you focus on problem solving you become the go-to person in your industry: the person of influence.

9. **Creating advocates.** You will have achieved influence when everyone else says so. The internet is awash with self-proclaimed experts or gurus on every topic known to man. Real influence is measured by the opinion of others who openly share your message and their opinion of you at every opportunity.

On more than a few occasions in interviews or during keynote presentations I've been asked *that* question: 'What is your secret to becoming an overnight success?' My answer is always, 'I don't know. I've never become that, or met anyone who has.' I have, however, met many people who, through persistence, focus and working to a plan, have been able to appear as though they transitioned from obscurity to highly influential overnight.

Throughout this book you will find case studies of real people who have used this exact process to make an incredible difference to their businesses and lives. They are every-day people from many different industries, and their stories showcase how you can also create amazing opportunities for yourself and your business. All of these amazing people completed my 12-Week Influencer Program. This book is about the principles of that program and the process it follows.

I believe this to be true, and I have also coached hundreds of people who have *proven* it to be true. If you follow the principles outlined in *Influencer* you will be ready to start creating a powerful position as an influencer in your industry in just ninety days.

These are my beliefs about influence, and the reason why you might just choose to elevate your own influence. Should you believe as I believe, or at the very least would like to explore the concept, this book is for you. Settle into your favourite reading place, and grab your notebook and pen. Your journey to becoming a person of influence starts here.

CHAPTER 1

My Story

The first step in writing a new book is always months of research. It seems like with each new book I write I spend more and more time in this phase, and *Influencer* was no exception.

I like to research more than just the topic. I'm always interested in asking what type of book the people who follow me on social media, or engage in the content I share, really want to read. When I asked this question of tens of thousands of people, I was surprised by their responses; not only the feedback on the question itself but also by the common thread running through the extra information they shared.

One of the hundreds of responses was this one: *Adam, I don't mind what book you write next, but what I would really love to read is your story, your journey that brought you to where you are and what you do today.*

I can say with complete honesty that I was a little shocked at first, not at the thought of including such personal information in my next book, but that anyone would be interested to reading about me. So I decided to stress test that suggestion.

I went back to social media and the many groups I am a member of to ask this question alone. Given that you are now reading this chapter I'm sure you realise that the answer I received was an overwhelming *yes* to include my story.

So here it is.

At the time of launching this book, I am fifty-four years of age. My journey to this point started when I was twenty-four and opened my first business on the Gold Coast in Queensland, Australia. I had decided to turn my hobby into a business, and opened a water and snow-ski shop with two good mates, Ray Wood and Stuart Harker. These two fine gents possessed greater wisdom than I, and I can say without a doubt that without their collective wisdom I would almost certainly have joined the huge percentage of small-business start-ups that fail within two years. However, survive and grow we did.

They were both silent partners, and so did not hold active roles within the business on a daily basis. The plain truth is that I had needed their wisdom, business experience and cash in equal measure to get started in my first business venture; that early experience taught me the value of mentors and coaches, and I have had both ever since.

Over the years both Stuart and Ray sold their shares back to me and went on to other successful ventures and careers. I met Ray through Stuart, and I want to acknowledge that Ray Wood has been one of the most important people to have guided my journey, starting with the first day that we met to discuss becoming business partners and going right through until today. He remains one of my closest friends, and has been a foundational rock in every facet of my life, personally, and also as a guiding light throughout my career. He has been there for me through some of the darkest days of my life, and has celebrated every win with me, which is why I have dedicated this book to him.

The world opens up

It was through this first business that I also found my passion for travel, and during the fourteen years that the business was a part of my life I travelled to Hong Kong, New Zealand, Japan, the United States and Canada. In particular, I went to the United States many times, often twice a year, to visit suppliers and attend trade shows.

Since those early days I have had the good fortune to travel overseas on more than seventy occasions and have visited twenty-four countries in this amazing world we live in.

My next business venture began during one of my trips to Orlando, Florida. I ran into former Australian world champion slalom skier Brett Thurley, whom I knew from the ski industry back home. At the time Brett was vice president of the Texas-based company Tige Boats and they were looking for an Australian distributor for their incredible brand of luxury wakeboard boats. Over a couple of dinners in Orlando with Brett and Tige's founder, Charlie Pigeon, Tige Boats Australia was born (www.tige.com).

By this time the water and snow-ski retail business had grown to three stores, and we had formed a partnership with Chris Grady of Brisbane-based business Waterskiers Connection. Chris and I purchased a third store in Brisbane, Waterskiers World. Over time I was able to become less focused on the retail businesses because Chris was doing such a great job running them, and devote more time to Tige.

Eventually the time came to exit the retail stores; two of these were sold to new owners, and Chris retained Waterskiers Connection. Chris and I remain good friends to this day.

Tige remained a big part of my life for a number of years until 2004, which was to prove a pivotal year. During 2004 my first wife and I separated, and in 2005 I sold Tige to my partners during our divorce, although I remained for a few more years as its CEO. This proved to be a bittersweet time, with so many changes happening in my life. The bitter part of this is best left untold, but the sweet part was marrying Julie, my beautiful wife of twelve years. Julie and I decided to have another child a couple of years after we married, and when Julie was pregnant with our daughter Tyla I left Tige.

I was about to become a dad once again. I have a son and daughter from my first marriage, Julie has two boys from her first marriage, and Tyla would make five children between us. At this point I had no business, no job and no idea what was next. We decided to focus on the impending arrival of Tyla and let the universe guide my next career move. And guide us in mysterious ways it did.

I found myself working on a movie set as a double for Gary Sweet, one of the lead actors in the movie *Chronicles of Narnia: Voyage of the Dawn Treader*. To say that Gary and I looked alike at the time is an understatement. The experience was a lot of fun, but I decided that a life in the movies was not for me.

It was, however, during this interesting time that I met Colin and Narelle Chenery, and Alf Orpen, owners of the company Organic and Natural Enterprise Group (ONEgroup), which I would join and be a part of for over six years. I fell in love with this company and its mission to produce some of the world's best certified-organic products, and maintain a focus on sustainability.

Discovering social media

It was during my time at ONEgroup that my passion for social media was born. The first of my two roles with the company was retail manager (I went on to become general manager). As retail manager, I researched companies around the world that operated in a similar way to ONEgroup in the production of its skincare lines, and I was interested in finding out what was the differentiator between companies that experienced rapid growth and those that did not. It turned out these companies were early adopters of social media, which convinced me that this social-media thing was here to stay, and that businesses of the future would need to master this relatively new phenomenon.

I should disclose that at this time, 2011, I knew absolutely nothing about social media. I had a Facebook account like most people, and probably looked at it once a week. Although I didn't know it at the time, this a-ha moment planted the seed that directed my life's journey and where I would go in the future.

My interest in social media started out as a focus on how it would help ONEgroup deliver the message of the importance of organic products and sustainability to the world. It quickly became my passion; Julie called it an obsession and she was probably correct, as she almost always is.

In my spare time, I did extensive research on social media, and as the general manager of a great business like ONEgroup I was able to reach out to some of the world's leading people in this area at the time, and leverage their knowledge and skills to further my own knowledge. This led to me consulting for and owning a share in a social-media business for a period of time.

Over time I became most interested in LinkedIn. It just made sense to me personally as my background was very much business focused, and getting to understand LinkedIn and how to best utilise it became my sub-passion. This passion for LinkedIn continues to this day.

I had also started to develop a small consulting business at this time. I had a few clients, and helped them mainly with their use of social media, but it was not much more than a hobby and gave me a little extra income.

In my opinion, this is where the story gets interesting, but you can be the judge.

LinkedIn changes everything

In 2013 I received a message on LinkedIn from someone who wanted to connect with me. I looked into his profile, and he seemed quite an interesting guy so I accepted his connection request. He was a business-development manager for a company based in Melbourne, but with offices in the UK, Singapore and the United States. We sent a few messages back and forth, just basic get-to-know-you stuff, and a few weeks later he suggested that I come to a dinner so we could meet face to face, and I could also meet the cofounder of his company, which was putting on the dinner for business owners in Brisbane, Australia. Brisbane is an hour's drive north of where I live, and I recall thinking twice about accepting the offer. However, accept I did.

On the day of the dinner, however, I had a long challenging day at ONEgroup and in the afternoon I made the decision to give the dinner a miss. I jumped in my car to head home that evening. I came to the intersection at the end of the street, where I usually turned right towards home. If I turned left, I would connect with M1 north to Brisbane.

The traffic on this evening was unusually heavy, and as I sat waiting at the intersection I had what I now refer to as my 'sliding doors moment'. This is a reference to the movie *Sliding Doors*. If you haven't seen it, it's about two alternative life journeys that are set in motion when Gwyneth Paltrow's character makes the decision to either step onto a train or not.

Turn right and go home to Julie and the children, or turn left and go to the dinner. I recall agonising over that decision. I had said I would attend, and I knew I should make the effort. The car basically steered itself: I turned left and headed for Brisbane. That decision would radically change the course of my life forever.

At the dinner, the speaker was Glen Carlson, cofounder of the business that, at that time, was called Key Person of Influence and today is known as Dent (www.dent.global). Glen's style was relaxed and his message resonated with me a great deal. We sat together for a time after the meal was served and got to know each other a little better. I agreed to come along to a one-day event he was running at the Brisbane Convention Centre a couple of weeks later.

The convention turned out to be one of the best I had ever attended. I caught up with Glen again that day, and we chatted some more about what I was doing in the social-media consulting space. The next step for me was to go to a more in-depth meeting about the program Key Person of Influence (KPI), a 40-week commitment and, at the time, an investment of a little over $10,000.

I was not going to make such a decision without speaking to Julie, and I headed home after a well-spent Saturday in Brisbane.

At this point, life got in the way as it tends to do, and I missed the next meeting.

Some weeks later, Glen called me out of the blue and said he was coming back to Brisbane and had some time for breakfast before returning to Melbourne. We agreed to meet at Sanctuary Cove, on the northern tip of the Gold Coast, Queensland. It was at this meeting that I decided to join the program.

I was now juggling a full-time role at ONEgroup, a small consulting business, a 40-week training program, and a family, which included a toddler who didn't seem to understand the concept of sleep. I soon discovered a new waking time each day of four am, which enabled me to get everything done.

Part of the KPI process was for each individual to write a book about their area of expertise; I now discovered a new waking time of three am, with some extra work on weekends and every evening.

I also discovered a new passion for writing. My first book, *Social Media Secret Sauce*, was launched. The KPI program was a real game changer for me, as was the publication of my first book. These two events combined set me on the path I am on today and most likely will be on for the rest of my life.

However, this pathway has more to add to the story; it set me on a trajectory to meet the two people who would become the most significant influencers in my life—apart from Ray Wood and the amazing Julie Houlahan.

Dr David Dugan (www.daviddugan.com) was one of the KPI mentors, and I learned a great deal from him. We became close friends throughout the course of the 40-week program. David also runs Abundance Global, which I am still a member of to this day. After the KPI program had finished, David invited me to be a speaker at one of his events to talk about my book, and social media in general.

Over time, David and I did more and more together, and in 2016 we decided to launch Web Traffic That Works (www.webtrafficthatworks. com) as a joint enterprise, and he remains my business partner, coach and close friend to this day. He was and still is an integral part of the success that our company has achieved on a global scale.

David also had a hand in one of the world's most respected mentors becoming my mentor and close friend. When David asked me to speak at his event, he said, 'Adam, there's someone coming to this event I want you to meet. Paul Dunn will be the other keynote speaker apart from you, so you'll get to spend some time with him over the two days.'

Paul Dunn, as I have mentioned, is an incredible mentor to many well-known names in the entrepreneur circles of Australia, the UK, US and New Zealand, a list that includes David Dugan, Glen Carlson and Glen's business partner Daniel Priestley, and many more. Paul is also a philanthropist and chairman of the global giving movement, B1G1 (www.B1G1.com).

To say that Paul and I had an instant rapport at David's event would be to understate those two days, and the impact Paul has had on my life since. In a phone call to Paul when he returned home to Singapore a week later, I described our meeting as being as impactful as seeing the births of my children, and it was.

Paul's guidance in my career and life journey since that day has been profound. One of his greatest impacts had been to open my eyes to the ability of businesses of any size to participate in philanthropic projects that make this world a better place. One of my greatest joys and proudest achievements is to have impacted the lives of over one million people through B1G1 and Web Traffic That Works (you can see more on this at www.webtrafficthatworks.com/impact).

All of which brings me to the present day. These days I spend my time travelling the world to speak at some amazing events, almost always about LinkedIn and the ways to leverage this platform from a personal and business perspective. You will read more about that in the coming chapters.

When I'm not travelling I'm based with Julie on the beautiful Gold Coast in Queensland, Australia. Four of our children have grown up and left school, and are now on their own life journeys. Tyla is the exception; she travels extensively with Julie and me.

You will often find me on board one of Royal Caribbean's ships, cruising the South Pacific. I spend a few days delivering keynote presentations to the passengers, and enjoy the cruise life the rest of the time. If you're ever on board one of these ships, please do come up and say hello. On many occasions I've had the great honour of meeting people from all corners of the world, who come up to me and say they have a copy of one of my books, or that we're connected on LinkedIn. It never gets tiring to meet people in this way.

You will also find me regularly working from a laptop in one the Gold Coast's many coffee shops, or on a park bench beside one of our many beautiful beaches (www.destinationgoldcoast.com). Our company, Web Traffic That Works, has an amazing team of superstars across the world who, like me, live a laptop lifestyle, and work with incredible entrepreneurs across the globe every day.

This is my story and my journey. I hope you enjoyed reading about it as much as I enjoyed sharing it with you, but now let's get into the true purpose of this book.

CHAPTER 2

The Value of Being Influential

'The key to successful leadership today
is about influence, not authority.'
—Ken Blanchard

Why would you want to be influential? This is a question I have asked now of over three hundred entrepreneurs, and understandably I hear a wide range of answers. There is, however, a common theme that stands out.

Bearing in mind that most people are referring to the way they succeed with their on-line marketing, personal branding, and of course their LinkedIn presence, the responses almost always revolve around the ease with which they can gain traction to fill webinars, live events and membership programs, and get face-to-face meetings with potential clients. The premise being that if you're seen to be highly knowledgeable in your industry, and in demand, people are more likely to want to hear what you have to say.

The agglomeration of these answers can be summed up in two words: *effortless sales.*

I agree with this premise, and with the concept that influence equals effortless sales, provided of course that the product or service is world class, and the way both are presented is clearly articulated and valued by whomever they are being presented to. More on this very soon, but for now let's stay focused on the first step, which is to be perceived as an influencer in an industry as outlined in the introduction.

Influence is best achieved through creating your personal brand, and there are a multitude of good books, courses and people willing to help you create yours. Everyone—your team, your clients and potential clients, and especially the media if you're seeking heavy exposure—will be swayed in their opinion of you through your personal brand. LinkedIn is one of the best platforms to develop that brand in two very important ways.

Firstly, LinkedIn gives you the opportunity to showcase yourself through imagery, i.e. your profile image, background image, and any other images or video you attach to your profile. Secondly, you can outline in words through the summary and experience sections everything about you, including what you stand for.

It's my belief, and also my experience, that the written content on LinkedIn is what will give you the greatest opportunity to create your brand. As mentioned, it can be done in the summary and experience sections, but equally important is the ability to create and share content, or express opinions on the platform. This is what will set you on your journey to influence, but so few people get it right and let me share why.

At the time of writing, there are four critical numbers that tell the story:

1. 550,000,000
2. 1,000,000
3. 100,000
4. 0.02 percent

The first number is an estimate of how many people are currently on LinkedIn, which is around 550,000,000 and this number is still growing by two additional profiles every second of every day of every week of every year. Taken in isolation, that might seem like a huge pool of people (and it is), so how on earth can you stand out in such a crowd?

The second number, 1,000,000, is again a rough estimate, and it relates to how many of those 550,000,000 profiles are *content creators*. This means that they create original content on a regular basis and post to either the publisher platform or as status posts, and it includes creators of video content. I will cover this in more depth in later chapters, but for now take my word for it that influence that comes from your content creation is the number one of all nine drivers.

The third number, 100,000, is a rough guide as to how many of these creators are generating the type of content that engenders influence.

I put it to you that if you know how to create the right type of content, and do this consistently, you have what I know to be an unprecedented opportunity to become one of the very few people—in fact, one of just 0.02 percent of all people on LinkedIn—with the ability to generate real influence and effortless sales. The good news is that by time you finish reading this book that is exactly what you will have, plus the other eight influence drivers. Combined, these influence drivers will form the roadmap for creating your pathway in the next ninety days to becoming an influencer for your business and in your industry.

I want to make it very clear at this point that I am not talking about what is termed 'influencer marketing'. I'll explain the difference between this and the *why*, and how you can become an influencer yourself.

Influencer marketing

You only have to do a search using the term 'influencer marketing' to find millions of articles on the subject, and this alone should tell you it's one of the hot topics or buzz phrases of our day. If you've read my previous book, *The LinkedIn Playbook*, you will have seen a similar distinction I made between social selling and social serving.

Influencer marketing is the practice whereby you leverage someone else's influence by engaging them to represent your brand. It is these people that your ideal clients or customers perceive as being credible— more so than you or your brand and business. The opinions and often buying habits of others are swayed by these people's endorsement of you. Influencer marketing is big business on Instagram, and is estimated to be worth in excess of US$2 billion in 2019 alone.

It is a niche area, and often people you have never heard of, and are unlikely to ever hear of, many of whom are school age, are at the low end of this practice, receiving free products, holidays, accommodation and so on up to the high end of the spectrum, which represents millions of dollars to align with brands. I personally endorse a number of companies as an influencer for their brands under this practice.

Again, let me be very clear: I have no issue whatsoever with influencer marketing, given that I participate in this practice regularly. But influencer marketing is very different to being an influencer within your industry.

Becoming an influencer

I won't be showing you a pathway to becoming an influencer in the above sense. I will be showing you a proven method that I have used myself, and many of the people I coach have used, to become influential within a microniche.

A microniche is centred on your personal experience or the business you use to generate revenue month after month, year after year. It's designed to place you firmly in the driver's seat, in control of your ability to generate income for yourself and your family. You set the price, you choose whom you work with, and you are seen as the person of influence within your industry.

That industry could range from global to local. The underlying premise is not to be using the term 'influencer', which is what many people are doing online these days, whether or not they actually are influencers. True influence is obtained when your market refers to you as such, not when you add this term to your website, LinkedIn profile or marketing copy.

Does this mean you cannot or should not take up or seek opportunities within the influencer-marketing juggernaut? It's entirely up to you to decide, if and when those opportunities present themselves. My methodology is about something more predictable and controllable than influencer marketing.

Is becoming an influencer in this sense the only way to market your business in the coming years? Of course not, and nor will it suit everyone. It could potentially be a great option for you, and you may still decide it's not your cup of tea. But at the very least you will have the information required to make the decision to jump right into the process, or explore different opportunities more suited to your choice of marketing.

Why might you choose to become an influencer in this way? I believe there currently exists a rare opportunity to do something very few people in the world are doing exceptionally well, which is to create new opportunities to market themselves and/or their businesses in a powerful way. I outline the process in detail in the coming chapters.

CHAPTER 3

The Three Drivers of Influence

There is a very simple framework to becoming influential, and it consists of three drivers and nine accelerators. Let's start with those three drivers, which form the basis of the nine accelerators:

Driver #1: Know
Driver #2: Like
Driver #3: Trust

In order for you to become influential, people have to undertake a journey with you. They first need to discover you: this is the *know*. Once they have discovered you, they then have to decide what they think of you and, more importantly, how they feel about what you stand for: this is the *like*. And finally, they have to have confidence in who you are, what you have to say, what you stand for, and your expertise: this is the *trust*.

How you create your influencer strategy has to, in the simplest of goals, take your tribe on this journey of discovery.

Before people can get to know you they first need to be able to find you, and this is where LinkedIn will become your best friend. You could spend thousands of dollars on a personal website and then thousands more in SEO strategies and or Adword campaigns every year to make sure your website is found in searches—or you could, at no cost, set up an exceptional profile on LinkedIn.

I've already shared with you how many profiles are on LinkedIn at the time of writing (550,000,000) and how this number is growing at a phenomenal pace. But remember that only 0.02 percent of LinkedIn profiles could be considered highly influential, and yet every day I still see so many profiles that are underwhelming and damaging to these people's personal brand. The very first step in this journey is to make sure you have an exceptional profile. This will be the first impression people have of you, and you have just a few seconds to make it great.

If you have a copy of *The LinkedIn Playbook*, you already have a comprehensive guide on how to do this to a high standard. If you have a copy but haven't yet updated your profile using the playbook methodology, I suggest you stop at the end of this chapter and get it done before moving on.

If you don't have a copy of *The LinkedIn Playbook* you can buy the paperback on Amazon. If you're happy with a PDF version, you're welcome to join my free group on Facebook: www.facebook.com/groups/LinkedIn2Success. All group members have access to a free download of the book.

If you prefer our team to do this for you, email us at clientdelight@ webtraffichatworks.com and we will outline our profile makeover service with you.

Driver #1: Know

At this point I will assume that you have an amazing profile on LinkedIn, or that you will have very soon. It's important that you do have because this is where you will give people the opportunity to get to know you.

Background image: There is one thing that will have great impact and give people the first opportunity to know who you are. It will do more than anything else to capture people's attention, and this is your background image. This is one of the most underused yet most visible representations of you.

We tend to absorb information in at least one of three ways: visual images, written content, or video. To use myself as an example, I'm not able to process video content very well; you only have to ask my wife Julie to know I cannot read a map to save my life. However, give me a step-by-step written process and I will follow it to the letter.

Make sure that people can experience all three; they will undoubtedly prefer one to another and you want to cover all bases. So make sure you have a great background image.

Written content: You have just 2,000 characters of text for your summary and your position descriptions, so use them wisely to present your written roadmap to those whose preference is to absorb information through the written word.

Video: Invest in a really good video that gives some context for who you are. I would suggest keeping it to around two minutes and certainly no more than three minutes.

Keywords: If you have followed the playbook methodology you will have included strong keywords that help LinkedIn show your profile to people during their searches. This will be one of your greatest friends with regard to free and targeted visibility on your profile, and it will be your first step in allowing people to get to know you. The next step is by your connection strategy, and the last step is through your amazing content. We will cover these topics in depth in coming chapters.

Driver #2: Like

Ask yourself this question: When was the last time you purchased anything from someone you really dislike?

Make yourself the first choice: There are times when we have no choice but to deal with people we dislike. As an example, in my previous home we had no option when it came to service providers for our home phone connection. No matter how little I liked this service provider (and I really did) if I wanted a home phone service I had to use them.

In most cases, however, we have a degree of choice, and likewise it's almost a certainty that you will not be the only option available in the service you provide. But even if you are, the long-term viability of your business will always be better if your clients love you instead of seeing you as the only option. I'm certain that if they do like you it will have some bearing on the purchasing decisions in the future.

Post online content wisely: I'm not suggesting that you need to undergo a personality transplant or change yourself in significant ways. But I am suggesting that you are careful about what you post on LinkedIn (this won't be an issue if you follow the content guide I will share in coming chapters). Of equal or perhaps more importance, you should also be careful about what you post on any other social-media profiles.

I personally know people who have lost job and client opportunities due to some less than savoury posts on platforms like Facebook, Instagram, Snapchat, and so on. You may recall that in 2018 Roseanne Barr's new TV sitcom was axed after an 'ill-worded' post caused condemnation all the way to the White House, and internationally.

I can assure you that once someone has decided to explore the option of engaging your services, they are highly likely to do a search on you and see what turns up.

If you haven't done a search on your own name recently, do it now. Open your favourite browser, type in your name and see what comes up online about you. Most likely you will find that any social media profiles you have will be readily available and anyone can access them from these search results.

You could choose to set some of your social-media profiles to private, and that would help somewhat if you decide it would not be to your advantage for people to see certain posts, but it will be a lot easier to become influential if you're not plagued by any untoward online content.

What I really mean by 'like' in this context is that people like the content you share online. This is as simple as ensuring that your content strategy is designed to appeal to a microniche of the market (we'll cover this in depth soon, too). The word 'like' also means that people find you open and engaging, and when you do share content they feel inclined to comment or share on your behalf.

Find your tribe: The best influencers engage with their tribe, and are respectful of the value and privilege involved in having people choose to express their opinions or praise of you. But choose your tribe wisely; you don't need everyone to like you, and there is real value in polarising your tribe. (This will be a future chapter of its own.)

Driver #3: Trust

In the words of Stephen Covey: 'Trust is the glue of life. It's the most essential ingredient in effective communication. It's the foundational principle that holds all relationships.'

You should now ask yourself another similar question to the last one: When was the last time you purchased anything from someone you really don't trust? There were probably near zero times you were okay with doing that.

Major brands spend millions of advertising dollars in the pursuit of trust in their brands, or in rebuilding it when they lose it. And while you don't need to spend a great deal on this, you do need to be perceived as trustworthy if your influence is going to be a revenue driver for you.

Stephen Covey wrote an exceptional book on trust called *The Speed of Trust*, and it has some great quotes. One of my personal favourites is: 'Over time, I have come to this simple definition of leadership: Leadership is getting results in a way that inspires trust.'

I put it to you that the word 'leadership' in this context is tantamount to influence; 'thought leader' is a well-worn phrase today and simply another way of saying influencer. If you seek effortless sales, look no further than trust. We know trust can easily be broken. Achieving a level of trust is necessary, but at the same time we know that the achievement of trust is a lifelong journey and not the end goal. There are, in my opinion, five pillars of building trust:

1. **Be the real you, always.** I have personally met many people that were influenced by at some point, whether it was through their sporting prowess, business acumen, or some other talent they were known for. The ones who really stick in my mind as being true influencers are the ones who were exactly the same in real life as the person I got to know, like and trust through the media and online though their content. Equally, my trust had been broken when I've come to the realisation that part of a person's public face was a show or a persona they created that was not the real them.

2. **Be honest.** I touched on the concept of polarising your tribe and will share an entire chapter on this soon. Honesty in your communication will build trust by polarising your followers, who will either agree or disagree with your viewpoint. Remember, you're not looking to appeal to everyone and it's okay to upset a few people along the way. People may not always agree with what you stand for, or your point of view, but they will respect your honesty.

3. **Stick to your superpower.** In other words, stay consistent to your tribe and your message. There's no easier way to lose trust than to be unclear in your message. Building trust in a niche is your objective, not trying to appeal to everyone.

4. **Play the long game.** Right now, I'm envisioning an image I've seen many times over the years. It's an image of a miner who has buried his pick in the dirt wall in front of him and walked away, giving up on his quest for gold. Just beyond his pick, a few centimetres away, is a rich vein that would change his life forever. Don't be the miner who quits right before that huge break. Stick with it and FOCUS (follow one course until successful).

5. **Give away your best knowledge.** In most cases, people want the solution more than the know-how to get it. When I released my last book, *The LinkedIn Playbook*, many people contacted me and said something along the lines of: *I can't believe you gave away the information on how to succeed on LinkedIn. Now nobody needs your help to do that. You're going to lose so much money.*

Of course, the opposite of this occurred. More people got to know who I was and reached out to me for those services. Thousands of people received (and are still receiving) great value from the process I shared, and many of them now refer their colleagues to my work.

Now you have the framework for creating influence, the three drivers of influence: know, like, trust. Each of these drivers has three accelerators, and I will now explain these nine accelerators in a step-by-step process so that you, too, can become that person of influence you desire to be.

CHAPTER 4

The Nine Accelerators
of Influence

Each of the three drivers of influence has three accelerators that will enable you to achieve it. The accelerators are outlined in a deliberate order. Follow them in this order to achieve the maximum benefit and best results from this entire process. As with the three drivers—know, like, trust—the accelerators are usually attained one after the other.

For the *know* driver, the three accelerators are:

1. Creating a micro-niche
2. Having an exceptional profile
3. Having a very clear message

For the *like* driver, the three accelerators are:

1. The ability to tell your story
2. Being able to engage your market
3. The content you share with your market

For the *trust* driver, the three accelerators are:

1. Becoming the problem solver
2. Building your community
3. Creating advocates

Of course, what this all means to each of us will vary, but the framework has been tried and tested many times over in multiple industries, countries and individual profiles. By profile, I'm referring to a simple online tool you can use to determine your own.

My personal favourite is the Wealth Dynamics profiling tool created by Roger Hamilton. There are eight profiles within Roger's framework, and we all fall under one of them. The profiles are mechanic, creator, star, supporter, dealmaker, trader, accumulator and lord. My own profile within the Wealth Dynamics framework is a lord.

No one profile is better than another. Each person's profile simply represents what they will find is their natural genius; in other words, what they do best. Many examples of well-known people are given in each category.

Before embarking on your journey to becoming an influencer, I highly recommend you use the Wealth Dynamics profiling tool to do this simple test, possibly the best investment in yourself you can make (if you've already taken the test there's no need to do it again). To read more about this tool and the many benefits you will get from knowing your profile, see https://wealthdynamics.geniusu.com.

The point of this test is to give you clarity on what is your natural genius and what comes easiest to you, or, as Roger puts it: 'Why make things hard work when you can follow your natural flow?'

I'm sure you're asking what this has to do with becoming influential, and it's a good question. The answer is that I know your success in this journey will be infinitely greater if you choose to become influential within the sphere of your natural talents; this is the path of least resistance.

Often this is the single greatest challenge the people I have now personally coached through this process have had to overcome. Many of these people chose to park the journey to influence until such time as they gained real clarity on the seemingly simple question I am about to ask you. It's the single most important, and therefore very first step, in your journey. It's also the reason why this is the very first of the nine accelerators, and will make or break the entire outcome for you. The question is: What is it that you want to be influential about?

Everything will flow in a logical order once you have answered this question honestly. In other words, this is your microniche. We will dive deeper into all the nine accelerators in later chapters, but for now my advice to you is to do your Wealth Dynamics test right now, before you read any further.

Once you have completed your test, and it should only take you thirty minutes to do, you will be equipped to read the next chapter, which covers the micro-niche in detail.

Once you have read chapter 5, I would put down this book until you have some real clarity on exactly what your microniche is, or could be. The remaining eight accelerators will be easier to put in place once this first step is clear in your mind. A word of warning: at the end of this process, when you have found out what your microniche is, you could find that you are in the wrong job, wrong business or wrong industry right now. All I can say is that it's far better to know that now, when you can start building your influence around something you truly love and will be passionate about for many years to come. It doesn't matter if you are fifteen or fifty, you have the time and ability to pivot from whatever you're doing right now to something that gives you real joy and satisfaction.

I was fifty-two years of age before I truly discovered what I wanted to do. It required a big shift in what I was doing on a daily basis, and in the business I had built only a few years prior. If I could do it at fifty-two, you can do it, too. Hopefully you will find that you're already in your flow and doing what it is you love to do, and your journey will be a breeze from here.

So, put this book aside now and either pull out your Wealth Dynamics report if you've already been through this process, or go to the URL I shared earlier and do your test. Once you have your report, really study it and understand the magic it's telling you about yourself. Then come back and read the next chapter.

Clarity Message

Steve Dart

Steve is a marketing and brand-strategy consultant. He specialises in assisting well-established businesses that are having difficulties in transitioning to a new digital, social and mobile world of business.

What was the biggest challenge you were having with LinkedIn before doing the 12-Week Influencer Program?
Understanding how to put it all together, and use LinkedIn as my primary resource for gaining attention leading to contract consideration from leading companies.

How has your time spent on LinkedIn changed since completing the program?
By implementing the strategies in the 12-Week Influencer Program I have moved from a mediocre executive profile to a premium engaged profile. I have also been very successful in connecting with the right type of people, leading to greater considerations and attention for my services.

Can you share one or two amazing benefits you have experienced since completing the program?
When I started the program I was employed as a sales and marketing executive for a Queensland business called Play Hard Sports Equipment, which manufactured sports equipment. The business had primarily an ad-hoc approach to its marketing, and all the marketing had to be on free services like Facebook, Instagram, YouTube and LinkedIn.

With direct learning from the program, LinkedIn became a huge sales (and consideration) generator, enabling me to build the PHS brand equity and open the opportunity pipeline for sales. The result was a dramatic uplift in revenue, leading to 44.7 percent ($2.1 million) growth in one year (after trading for twenty-five years) and securing sports-equipment acquisition for the XXI Commonwealth Games Gold Coast.

How has this impacted you, either personally or as results for your business?

I gained the confidence to transition from employee to now taking on the biggest challenge of my life by starting my own marketing-and-brand-consultancy business. With the learning from over twenty-five years in sales and marketing, coupled with the newly acquired information from the 12-Week Influencer Program, I'm feeling unstoppable in building a mutually beneficial and productive partnership with all businesses that I will work with into the future.

Steve Dart

www.linkedin.com/in/steve-dart

www.dartmarketing.com.au

CHAPTER 5

Creating Your Microniche

Let's start by getting clear on exactly what a microniche is. To do that I'm going to use two good friends of mine as examples: Jason Malouin and Shane Saunders.

Jason is a photographer, and a great one at that. Many people who know his work can spot his headshots and know he was behind the camera without having to ask because his way of capturing an image on camera is so distinct.

If I was to ask you what Jason's niche is, you would likely say photography and you would be correct. But in terms of influence, a niche is too broad, and we need to drill down into that niche to narrow the focus. For Jason to dominate the entire photography niche he would be competing against every form of photography that exists, including aerial, fashion, pinhole, landscape, cityscape, nature, wildlife, wedding, black and white, travel, underwater, sunrise/sunset, storm, bird and portrait, just to name a few. Becoming influential in such a broad sense is extremely difficult.

Jason's superpower, what he is known and highly respected for, is headshot photography. This is his microniche, upon which he has built his influence. You can meet Jason on LinkedIn at www.linkedin.com/in/jasonmalouin.

Shane Saunders is a coach, and not just any coach; specifically, he is a breathing coach. He doesn't coach people in sports, mindset, business, music, cheerleading, life, wellness, career, relationships, sales or motivation. Although these all come under the niche of coaching, Shane is a breathing coach. That's right, he trains entrepreneurs to breathe properly so they can achieve what Shane calls 'peak state'. Shane's niche is coaching, and his microniche is breath coaching for entrepreneurs.

Shane is my breathing coach and I can tell you from experience that his has been one of the most impactful training programs I have ever undertaken. You can meet Shane on LinkedIn at www.linkedin.com/in/shane-saunders.

You can see from these examples that a microniche is a niche within a niche. Photography is a broad niche and headshot photographer is a laser-focused microniche. Coach is a broad niche and breathing coach for entrepreneurs is a laser-focused microniche.

Like Shane, I am also a coach, and given my previous books my niche is probably social media. Of course, that's much too broad. You could refine that to being an authority on LinkedIn, but again that's too broad. After all, there are many well-respected and talented people in the world who also know how to leverage LinkedIn like I do.

For me, a niche could be coaching influence, but that category should also be narrowed down. I would say that my microniche is more specific than that: I coach people to be influential using LinkedIn.

What is your microniche?

By now I have asked this question of the people I coach in our 12-Week Influencer Program hundreds and hundreds of times. Often it's not easy to see the micro-potential within a category. One such industry is real estate agents. The question asked by real-estate agents is usually: How much more niched can I be than to say I'm a real estate agent focused on residential properties?

Residential real estate is a broad niche. An example of a microniche within that broad niche could be specialising in finding under-priced residential investment properties in Brisbane between $700,000 and $1 million for investors with self-managed super funds. This microniche will move the real-estate agent out of the crowded space of the real-estate industry.

As we move through the other eight accelerators, you will see that it becomes easier to create content, have a clear marketing message, and build a specific tribe or advocates than if the niche was simply residential real-estate agent.

As an FYI, there are over 250,000 real-estate agents currently on LinkedIn. How many people who specialise in finding under-priced residential investment properties in Brisbane between $700,000 and $1 million for investors with self-managed super funds are there?

Now you have four clear examples of microniches: Jason, the headshot legend; Shane, the breathing coach; Adam, the influence-on-LinkedIn dude; and a real-estate agent that is your go-to guy for investment properties in Brisbane.

I can almost hear you thinking up your next question, and yes, we have covered that question hundreds of times, too. It's something along the lines of: *But if I only focus on headshot photography, or investment properties between $700,000 and $1 million, won't I be missing out on lots of opportunities in other forms of photography or real estate, and what happens if I find a great investment property for someone that is only $600,000?*

There is a well-known saying that covers this: 'If you try to appeal to everybody you appeal to nobody.'

Jason does plenty of photo-shoots of people that are more than just headshots, Shane makes a ton of money from group-based corporate-training days. I do a lot more than just coach influence on LinkedIn (in fact, our main revenue comes from managing the LinkedIn profiles of highly influential people). And even our real-estate agent sells plenty of properties for less than $700,000 or more than $1 million, and to homeowners as often as investors.

The point of the microniche is to make you stand out in a crowded space, and to make it much easier to be influential within that chosen space. Finding your microniche will rarely hinder you; in fact, I would say that in almost all cases it will grow your revenue.

The best type of microniche will combine your greatest passion (something that is in your natural flow as long as it's something you can generate an income from), with the opportunity to create a business, product or service around that passion. It's the intersection of passion, expertise and opportunity.

The Wealth Dynamics profile test

In the last chapter I suggested you take the Wealth Dynamics profile test if you have never done so before. The point of the exercise is to fully understand what flow means for you. Like most of us, you probably have more than one passion, and the test will help you hone in on a particular passion that you already have a great talent for. It will also help you build your knowledge around that natural flow and love for your chosen area of expertise.

Before jumping right in and being one hundred percent convinced that this passion is your chosen path, or your calling, ask yourself another question: Can I build a business, product or service that will monetise my passion? It will need to be within your ability to generate income from this passion. Otherwise you risk splitting your time between your non-paying passion, and the day job that generates your income. Or worse, going slowly broke while loving what you do every day.

I've met many successful entrepreneurs who make a good living but have no sense of fulfilment in their careers, or joy in their lives, because they have always been in pursuit of the money that comes from what they do. I have also met many people who live for their passion, but struggle to pay the bills because they haven't developed a powerful way to productise their gift. Believe me, you don't want to be in this space.

In the last chapter I also suggested that you read to the end of this chapter and then put the book aside until you have a rock-solid grasp of the microniche you want to move forward with. You also need to have an idea of the product, service or business you want to develop. It could be exactly what you're doing right now, and if that's the case then read on and get the next steps done as quickly as you can.

If you're not living your passion right now and want to use this book to take the first steps in this journey, my best advice is not to get too concerned about having everything in place in the next ninety days. Take your time to really consider this next step and get it right.

Most likely you'll find that you're not the first person to come up with your idea. That doesn't mean you should throw it out and look for something you've never done before.

If we take the example of our real-estate agent, would it matter if someone else were doing something similar in Sydney, New York or London? The price point in those examples would likely be much higher than $700,000, but no, it wouldn't matter at all.

What matters is that you choose something you are truly passionate about, enough to spend many of your waking hours doing, that you can generate an income from, and that it gives you the opportunity to own this space in your city or your industry.

Once you have your passion, and are considering how you might productise it, do some global research. You will probably find that someone has done it before you. While I'm not suggesting that you replicate their product or service, it should give you some comfort to know that you can create a marketable and viable product.

If you can't find even one example of someone doing something the same, or similar, to what you're considering I suggest you think hard about it. The world is full of people with a great idea before its time. Don't be the property developer who builds a new subdivision five years before the market is ready for it.

Hopefully, you already have a fair idea of what you plan to do from here or, even better, that you're lucky enough to already be doing it. From this point on, I'm going to make the assumption that you have this step sorted. Each of the following chapters should be read on the basis that you have clarity about what it is you will be building your influence for.

Clarity Message

Geoff Hetherington

Geoff is an advisory board chair, business educator, coach and mentor. On the surface he seems to wear many hats, but as you'll see from his profile he's best known as 'the clarity coach'. Geoff is a rare breed; his ability to communicate complex subjects in simple analogies makes it a breeze to understand what he's talking about.

Geoff is creating some of the best video content I see on LinkedIn, and gaining high-quality traction from his overall LinkedIn activity. If anyone has the ability to position himself as an influencer on LinkedIn, it is Geoff. This is what Geoff had to say after his 90-day journey through the influencer program.

What was the biggest challenge you were having with LinkedIn before doing the 12-Week Influencer Program?
I had lost interest in LinkedIn. I was very active for a couple of years, but I wasn't seeing any real results and was getting tired of all of the MLM approaches. I had pretty much written it off as a tool for recruiters and salespeople. Reading your book, *The LinkedIn Playbook*, convinced me that what I was missing was a plan of attack and some education about how to go about getting results.

How has your time spent on LinkedIn changed since completing the program?
I spend structured time with a clear plan of what I need to do to achieve the results I want, and I'm expanding my range of contacts and sales leads for potential clients.

Can you share some benefits you have experienced since completing the program?

I have new clients that I can attribute directly to my LinkedIn activity, both here in Australia and around the world, even one in Germany. I've increased my number of weekly views and am working to build my image as an influencer.

How has this impacted you, either personally or as results for your business?

For my business it means that I'm starting to attract attention from and communicate with potential clients at the level I'm after, and personally I like the slowly increasing number of people who are reading what I put up.

Geoff Hetherington

https://www.linkedin.com/in/geoffhetherington

www.theclarityceo.com

CHAPTER 6

Your Influencer Profile

I believe that one of the most important tools everyone, from the age of eighteen upwards, can invest in is their LinkedIn profile, regardless of whether they choose to use that presence to become an influencer in the sense of what I'm sharing in this book or not. There are three reasons to consider a LinkedIn profile.

1. **It's free.** Unlike creating your own personal website, which, even if you possess the skills to do it yourself, entails hosting expenses, and ongoing expenses for ownership of your domain name/s. Granted, these costs can be quite minimal, but getting visibility onto your site will not be. You will either need to invest significant personal time in search-engine optimisation (SEO) efforts or pay a professional for their time to do so. Anybody can set up a LinkedIn profile at no charge, and almost always that profile will be the top search result when people check you out online.

2. **You are not alone.** Over half a billion people currently have a profile, with two new profiles appearing every second of every day. LinkedIn's internal goals are for three billion people to have a

presence on their site. If you think you're late to the party, think again. If you don't already have one, the best day to set up your profile is today.

3. **It's easy to do.** Realistically, you can have an acceptable presence within a few hours. Every one of those current and future three billion profiles has access to exactly the same tools and format that you do. Whether they are the world's best-known industry heavyweights or eighteen-year-old students completing their final year of school.

Creating an exceptional profile

Everyone can have all-star status as part of their LinkedIn profile, but that flash-sounding category simply means they have completed all the sections of their profile. It doesn't necessarily mean that they've completed them well. It is, however, important to make sure that you do have an all-star profile to ensure that LinkedIn shows you the best searches.

Creating an exceptional profile will take a little more effort, but it's essential if you wish to become an influencer so let's dive right into that process now.

If your profile status is *Beginner*, *Intermediate*, *Advanced* or *Expert*, it's an indication that you've missed one of the eleven important steps (I will cover these in depth shortly). To update these first five areas, you need to go to your home page and click on the pencil icon in the upper-right area just below the background image. This will give you access to the following categories, all of which you will need to complete:

- Background image
- Profile image
- Headline
- Current position
- Education
- Country
- Zip code
- Locations within this area
- Industry
- Contact info
- Summary media

Now let's dive a little deeper into the critical ones.

1. **Background image:** This is the very top section of your profile and by default it's set to the standard light blue image you will see on many profiles. No influencers will leave this section on the default setting. It's imperative that you create a personalised background image to replace the default setting. If you have some reasonable skills in graphic design you can certainly give this a go yourself. If not, Canva (canva.com) is a great online tool you might choose to use to create your background image.

The dimensions you need to use can be found by going to your home page and clicking on the pencil icon in the upper-right area of the background image. This will give you the most up-to-date dimensions required since LinkedIn tends to change these occasionally.

You should also take note of where your profile image is currently displayed because this will appear over any text or images you have on your profile image. So make sure you format your background image with this in mind.

I highly recommend that you outsource this process to a professional graphic designer. If you don't have a relationship with someone who can do this, you can easily connect with someone who specialises in these on sites like Fiverr (www.fiverr.com) or Freelancer (www.freelancer.com).

I also suggest you spend some time scrolling through different profiles on LinkedIn until you find one or two that you personally resonate with and then brief your designer according to the style of image you would like. Another option would be to use something similar to your company or personal website home page, if appropriate, to keep alignment with your branding.

2. **Profile image.** Equally as important as the background image is your profile image. The best type of image is a headshot of yourself. Under no circumstances should this be a logo of your business, which should be part of your background image.

This is something you may choose to do yourself, but it's also worth spending a few hundred dollars for a professional photographer.

If you do decide to use something you already have, or a friend or family member has shot for you, ensure that it's shot in a well-lit area with a clear background. It's highly unlikely that the selfie you took on the weekend is going to be good enough quality, and always keep in mind that this is the first impression of you that people will have.

I also suggest you update this every couple of years at the least. There's nothing that destroys the trust factor (see later chapter on this) quicker than having a face-to-face or online meeting with someone you've connected with, only for them to find that you're ten or more years older than your profile suggests, or significantly heavier or lighter in weight, or you now sport a new beard, or are clean shaven, or have a completely new hair colour or style.

Believe me, I'm speaking from experience in all of these examples. It's imperative that you update your profile image if any of these examples are relevant for you now or in the future.

3. **Headline.** This is the area directly under your profile image and is one of the areas most likely to be read on your profile. This is your opportunity to give people a good first impression of what you're all about and why they might want to connect with you. I recommend completing this section in one of two ways. You could write a short sentence that outlines who you best serve and how you serve them, using specific keywords that showcase your areas of influence and expertise. Or you could use a mixture of both, which you will often find is how mine is showing. You only need to have a very small character count to use here—120, to be exact—so you need to be succinct and clear in your message.

4. **Contact info.** You need to click the pencil icon on the right to access this area. Once you're there, the first item to update is your profile URL. Again, by default LinkedIn will give you a terrible profile URL with a whole string of irrelevant numbers on the end.

    Click the link to your URL, which will take you to another page with your public profile settings. In the top right you'll see the section to edit and personalise your URL. Click the pencil icon here; you can change your profile URL to anything you choose as long as it's not being used by somebody else. I would make this as simple and short as you can (mine is now www.linkedin.com/in/adamhoulahan).

    While you're in this section, the next thing to do is click the option to make your profile visible to the public. You should also make public every aspect of the profile you can see here. Even if you only intend to operate in one country, activate the machine-translated profile option.

    Once you're finished here, return to the contact information section and complete as many of the options to have your details open to the public as you are comfortable with.

5. **Summary.** Again, this is one of the most important areas to utilise well. The character count here is just 2,000 and you'll likely need every one of them. I suggest you take a look at mine as an example, but here's the framework we use to create this section:

    *   Name
    *   Claim to fame
    *   Insight

- Elevator pitch
- Experience
- Problems your clients face
- How you solve those problems
- Personal *why*
- Call to action

This is a lot to cover, so you'll need to be succinct and spare the buzzwords.

I'm still surprised by how many people leave this section blank, or do a very poor job of giving people visiting their profile the opportunity they need to get to know them. Make this your best work, or outsource to a professional copywriter.

You also have the opportunity to add links to websites or videos below your summary. Take the opportunity to add at least two pieces of high-quality external media that highlights your expertise and what you do.

Once you've completed this section you can click the blue Save tab at the bottom and move onto the next sections.

6. **Experience.** This is the area most people use to list every job they've ever had, back to when they had a paper run as a student. You will use this very differently. This is where your profile will really stand out from the hundreds of millions of profiles that will never generate influence or revenue for their owner.

Once again, to gain an insight into what I outline here take a look at my profile. You'll see very little previous job history; although I mention in my summary that I've run six businesses throughout my career, there's no mention of most of them except my current business, Web Traffic That Works. What you will see in support of this business is what creates influence, my books, and my training program and our group.

I highly recommend that you do something similar. Have one entry about your business, and one about your product or service. If you've written a book, add another entry that outlines information about the book, provided it has some alignment with your business, product or service.

Again, just like your summary, you only have 2,000 characters, but you now have 2,000 characters for each of the sections you add as part of your experience. You can use these to outline what your past experience, or you can use them to go more deeply into what you do now and your real expertise.

I have already mentioned, but it's worth stating again, that in this area, where everyone on LinkedIn has the opportunity to do as they please, more than 99 percent do what everyone else is doing. Consequently they miss the potential this simple process can give them to become influential in their industry, using LinkedIn as their platform.

7. **Education.** You need to complete this section or your profile will not be 'all star'. It doesn't have to contain your formal education, but be sure to add your best two or three entries. You can also add links to media or websites here if you choose.

8. **Skills and endorsement.** This area is one of the most misunderstood LinkedIn profile options. You absolutely need to activate this area of

your profile, and you need to choose your skills wisely. Don't think of them as skills you may possess, such as hobbies or job skills. Instead, think of them as keywords you would want people to use in their searches. The top three are your most important since they are visible on your profile to people who come across you or choose to search for you. The rest are there to be viewed, but visitors will have to click the Show More tab to access them.

9. **Accomplishments.** In this section you have many options, and I don't suggest that you complete all of them simply for the sake of having them on your profile. Choose the ones that will help position you as both credible and influential—with one exception: languages. Make sure this one is active. The rest of the optional inclusions:

- Publication
- Certification
- Patent
- Course
- Project
- Honours and awards
- Test score
- Organisation

If you've written a book or books, or even had an industry paper published, list them here. The same goes for any awards, which are well worth showcasing.

10. **Interests.** These are broken into three categories:

- LinkedIn influencers
- Companies
- Groups

Any of these you choose to follow on LinkedIn will appear here, so make sure they're in alignment with your beliefs or, more importantly, the beliefs you want to have on show to the public.

11. **Recommendations.** There is another important section of your profile, and that is recommendations. This is covered in depth in a later chapter, but for now it's essential to know that you should have an ongoing strategy to increase your recommendations on your profile. There's no magic number of recommendations to have, but there is one number you don't want and that is zero.

You can only receive recommendations from people you are connected to on LinkedIn as first-degree connections. I don't recommend that you engage in the practice of swapping recommendations (i.e. I'll do one for you if you do one for me). There is no credibility in doing this, and keep in mind also that anyone viewing your recommendations can link to all the profiles of the people who have given them, as well as those you have given to others.

On occasion, people will voluntarily do you the honour of giving you a recommendation. If you've gone out of your way to create an exceptional outcome for a client, by all means ask them if they would be open to supplying a recommendation on your profile. If you click on their profile link, you will find an option in the More section to request a recommendation. Make it easy for them by sending them a request for one here. It will also give you the option to select how you have worked together.

Follow these eleven steps and you will have the exceptional profile that all influencers have, or at least should have.

At the end of the book there is a section titled My Gifts to You, in which there is a link to access a free e-book version of my previous publication, *The LinkedIn Playbook. This earlier publication* has some extra details on profile optimisation that you might want to access.

If this is something you would like some high-level assistance with, my team are on hand to assist you in that. For more information and details email clientdelight@webtrafficthatworks.com and someone will be in touch to give you the details about this service.

Clarity Message

Carolyn Butler-Madden

Carolyn is a marketing consultant specialising in social-purpose strategies and cause marketing. She is a bestselling author and the managing director of Sunday Lunch, a marketing consultancy specialising is cause-led marketing. They work with businesses that want to build more meaningful brands that stand for more than just profit. I'm personally a big fan of her work.

What was the biggest challenge you were having with LinkedIn before doing the 12-Week Influencer Program?

My content strategy wasn't working; I had very low engagement on posts and articles.

How has your time spent on LinkedIn changed since completing the program?

I have radically changed how I use LinkedIn since doing the program. Before, I took a very ad hoc approach, sharing other people's content and sharing my blog posts. I had no consistent approach to inviting people to connect with me.

I now post my own original content frequently, at least twice a week, and this is mainly short posts but also videos and some articles. One of the unexpected benefits has been that I've really found my voice. My confidence in expressing my opinion on things publicly has soared, and the feedback I've got from my connections as well as people outside of my direct network has increased that confidence. As a result, LinkedIn has now become my main platform for building my profile, and generating awareness about what I do and why it's valuable. It's become a great way for me to educate my network on the value of a social-purpose approach for brands.

I've also started using LinkedIn as a lead generation platform. I now use LinkedIn's tool, Sales Navigator, to target my ideal clients and invite them to connect. I've taken a slow and steady approach, and so far have increased my connections by about forty percent. And I've developed an approach to nurture my new connections by offering them value.

Can you share one or two amazing benefits you have experienced since completing the program?

As a direct result of my activity on LinkedIn, I've had two invitations to speak, one at a conference in Edinburgh, and another to a prestigious post-graduate management and business school. And I've received invitations to be interviewed on two podcasts, one in Australia and the other in the US.

But probably the biggest benefit is the sales process LinkedIn has created for me. LinkedIn is now the foundation of my sales process. Given the high value of my core product, it takes some time to nurture leads through my sales funnel.

How has this impacted you, either personally or as results for your business?

The unexpected benefit has come from posting my own content and opinions consistently. This has been a way for me to really find my voice and express my opinions confidently. That's been of huge value to me.

Another impact has been my increased profile, so now when I meet people or reach out, they're far more open to me than previously, and there have been times when people have said they've heard of me.

Carolyn Butler-Madden
www.linkedin.com/in/carolynbm
www.sundaylunch.com.au

CHAPTER 7

A Clear Message

'I resent the idea that people would blame
the messenger for the message, rather than
looking at the content of the message itself.'
—Anita Hill

There is a final piece of the puzzle in the first phase of having people get to really know you, and this is to have a clear message about who you are and what is the value proposition you represent. Most importantly, it clarifies exactly what the problem is that you solve. There is an entire chapter on this to come, but for now it's enough to know that your profile needs to be crystal clear on this.

Once you have an excellent LinkedIn profile that tells the story of who you are, who you help, the problem you solve, and a little about how you go about that, you should have a tight niche. This will help attract the people who are most likely to be interested in you and your solutions, and the content you will soon create that showcases your expertise in this area.

It's highly likely that people will start checking out your profile and discovering your content, and increasingly they will want to access more in-depth information about your services.

I often see many people on LinkedIn who have done the hard work to create interest in their profiles, and their solutions fail spectacularly at this important step. I've lost count of how many TV commercials I've watched without being able to recall afterwards what they were promoting or even what the business was. I've met people who cannot explain what they do for a living. I'm sure you have experienced this too. You don't want to be like those TV commercials or those people.

On the flip side of this are those advertisements that try to pack in every buzzword and as many messages as possible into thirty seconds, thinking they need to get the biggest possible bang for their buck. Or that guy at the networking event who, when asked the inevitable question ('So, what do you do?') replies with a well-rehearsed response that sounds like it was written by someone else and is completely lacking in authenticity. Worse still are those people who use so much jargon or 'big' words that nobody understands what they're on about. Once again, you don't want to be one of those people.

Moving from first view to client

Your clear message is about the next step people will take when they have been through the entire journey: *know, like, trust.* There will certainly be people, if there are not already, who will reach out to you directly through interaction with your content. Or they might send a direct message on your profile asking for an appointment with you, or for directions on how to find information.

This is normal activity, and takes place on my profile every week. However, while this is the outcome you want, the majority of people will still want to access more detail before doing so.

This next step is your opportunity to go much deeper than your LinkedIn profile allows. Use video content and written content that walks your new visitor through a clear pathway leading to whatever the best next step is. There is a saying in marketing that I believe in very strongly: Each marketing message you create has just one purpose: to sell the next message.

This goes back to what I alluded to previously. Many LinkedIn profiles fail spectacularly in moving people from interest to becoming a client, or from a cold lead to a warm one and then to a client. The mistake these profiles make is in trying to sell the outcome instead of the next step.

If your product or service is worth hundreds of dollars then this step can be shorter, but if people are required to invest thousands of dollars, or make a recurring monthly investment, it is very unlikely that they will progress from having found you on LinkedIn to becoming a client in one step. Once your profile has done its job and attracted interest, your next step will be crucial in turning an abundance of warm leads into clients. Otherwise those people will simply move onto the next person who does this step better than you.

Selling the next step

And now we come to the nugget of gold in this chapter: ensure your next message sells the next step. This will vary for each individual, but that next step will probably fit into one of these five categories:

1. Webinar
2. Phone call
3. Online meeting (Skype, Zoom, etc)
4. Face-to-face meeting
5. Any of the above with someone on your team

Work out which of these options will be the appropriate next step for you, and then craft your message around it (or brief your copywriters to do this for you).

Now that you're thinking of the 'message' as a series of logical next steps, work out how many steps you need to move people from simply viewing your profile and consuming the content to becoming clients. This is often referred to as the 'funnel'. Funnels can be quite generic in nature, so it's up to you to make yours specific, just like your niche.

To illustrate this point, I will use the example of a campaign we recently created for one of our clients.

The objective was to move people from being merely content consumers on LinkedIn to signing up for a training program at $19,000 per participant. These are the messages that took place:

1. LinkedIn content positions the CEO as highly influential in this industry to gain visibility on the profile
2. Profile outlines the service more than the business itself
3. Profile leads interested people to access more information about the service online
4. A direct message leads people to attend an upcoming, live half-day free event
5. Half-day event gives great value and invites people who want to explore the opportunity of the main program to book in for a small, group information session
6. Small group session gives a complete outline of the program and expected outcomes, and the opportunity to sign up to the program on a payment plan over ten months

As you can see, instead of directing people to a page that explained the program, each step simply sold the *next* step, which gave people the opportunity to move at their own pace, starting with finding our client on LinkedIn and finishing with investing $19,000.

Let's focus on just one step: moving from engaging with you on LinkedIn to choosing to seek more information elsewhere. You can direct people with some very simple next steps, using the powerful tools on LinkedIn that will help you elevate yourself above the masses, which is exactly what every good influencer does.

The first option is to direct people to your website. It's very easy to add a link to your communications and on your profile that directs people to your website. This is one of the simplest and quickest options to make more information available about your services, including information on why you created your website in the first place.

If you plan to do this, it's extremely important that your website has a clear message about the value you provide, and that it's congruent with your LinkedIn message.

When potential new clients reach out to me, the first thing we do is to see if we are a good fit for them and vice versa. The first step is to look at their website to get a better understanding of them and their services. It is often the case that their websites are confusing and, even worse, not aligned with their niche.

If you haven't updated your website in a while it will be worth your while, as part of this journey, to do so now, taking care to ensure that you have congruency with your niche.

Alternatively, a quick fix could be to create a new page on the website that focuses entirely on your niche. Instead of directing people to your home page, you could direct them from LinkedIn to this page instead.

Either way, keep in mind that whatever people are viewing at this point, there must be a clear message, and that message will be promoting the next step.

From there you will need to have your multi-stepped funnel in place, with a clear message for each of the subsequent steps in your customer's journey.

PointDrive

Directing people to your website is a valid option and it will get results, but I believe there is a better option available to you as a soon-to-be

LinkedIn influencer. Very few people utilise this option, so it will put you in the less-than-one-percent club at the top of the pack.

Sales Navigator is a separate subscription to your standard LinkedIn subscription, and technically speaking they are even separate platforms though of course they are integrated. PointDrive is a powerful add-on to Sales Navigator.

With LinkedIn alone, you can get basic insights into who has viewed your profile, and who has liked or commented on your content. You can also get low-level data on those people's professions and locations; however, it is extremely basic information.

With PointDrive, however, you can see exactly which presentations people view, how many times they have viewed it, and, most importantly, it will give you detailed information about where their focus was within your presentations. Did they watch your video? Did they watch it more than once? How much time in total did they spend on the page itself? How much time on each resource with the page? Where exactly is the viewer located? What type of devices do they use? What browser are they using?

As any sales professional will agree, getting this level of data about someone prior to having a meeting of any kind is extremely valuable information. As is the ability to tailor information to send to the potential client prior to the meeting, and all delivered with the click of a URL.

Using PointDrive, you can build incredibly detailed and user-friendly resources, and multiple versions of those resources. They are customisable; you have the ability to embed as maps, videos, PDF documents, and PowerPoint presentations. You can create a presentation that is specific to one client, or make it a generic resource. There are endless ways of using these presentations. A feature I love about PointDrive is being notified immediately when someone views your presentation.

If you are serious about using LinkedIn to generate business, you will need to invest in Sales Navigator as a minimum. You could get by using email and websites or landing pages, but the best of the best use Point Drive. It allows you to have all of your important information—your name, company, contact details, etc—at the very top of your profile. You can even have a different profile image if you like. These are the basic features of the tool. But PointDrive's real value lies in the insights it will give you into the people who visit your PointDrive presentations.

LinkedIn has great resources, tutorials and demonstrations, and you can request one of their team to go through the features of PointDrive with you so I won't go into a higher level of detail here. You can, however, go to this presentation I have built that explains how you can use PointDrive as part of your high-level clear-message strategy: https://ptdrv.linkedin.com/qgsifr0.

Hopefully, by now you are getting some real insights into the power of clear messaging, and how critical it is to the success of your influencer journey. If you don't already have them, I suggest you invest some time in building these assets as part of this journey. Keep in mind that you are investing ninety days in a process of launching yourself onto the world stage as a highly influential person in your chosen industry.

This is where a good portion of that time should be invested. You may want to park progressing further through this book until you build these assets in readiness for the next steps.

We have now come to the end of the first influence driver, which is to get people to *know* who you are, see the value of what you bring to the table, and understand why they might want to find out more. If you have followed the process up to this point, by now you should have a world-class profile, a laser focus on your microniche, and understand the importance of that microniche. You will also have a very clear message, using exceptional resources to deliver that message in a way that very few other people are doing right now.

At this stage, you will be at the pointy end of the power users on LinkedIn.

It's now time to delve into the process of getting your growing list of followers and connections to really 'LIKE' everything about you and move another step through their customer journey.

Clarity Message

Shane Saunders

Shane is a breathing coach, and he is also my breathing coach (I have shared more information about Shane elsewhere in the book). What Shane does has had a profound effect on me as a person and as an entrepreneur. If you asked Shane what he does, he would probably say this: 'I guide high-performing business leaders to get more energy and enhanced thinking so they can serve with excellence and sustained enthusiasm.'

What was the biggest challenge you were having with LinkedIn before doing the 12-Week influencer program?

I was always mindful that LinkedIn was for professionals, so I was scared to use the platform initially. I was afraid that what I had to offer on LinkedIn was not relevant and that somehow everyone on there must already know this stuff. I had a belief, like many people, that someone would find out that I didn't know what I was talking about. And I didn't want to cold-call market to my connections on there as I know I don't like it when people cold-call market to me.

How has your time spent on LinkedIn changed since completing the program?

I now get the concept of social serving, and being in the influencer program has been significant in defining my content so I can find and talk to the people and clients that want to be talking to me, versus me just marketing to everyone and anyone.

Can you share one or two amazing benefits you have experienced since completing the program?

The influencer program was a significant catalyst for the creation and release of our Virtual Breathing Space. The connection and marketing strategy I learned and then created has us on track to hit our first target to have the Virtual Breathing Space generating $40,000 a month in recurring revenue.

How has this impacted you, either personally or as results for your business?

The impact on me personally has been profound. It's been instrumental in the reduction of my 'imposter syndrome'. I now feel solid in my passion, and how I express who I am and what I do. The influencer program has helped me stay on the path to my purpose.

Shane Saunders

www.linkedin.com/in/shane-saunders

https://breatheme.com

CHAPTER 8

Stories and Why They Matter

'The shortest distance between truth
and a human being is a story.'
—Anthony de Mello

If you look back at some of the most successful ad campaigns of the past few years, most likely they were focused on telling stories. Adidas and Lionel Messi is a great example, as was the Mercedes Benz 'easy driver' campaign during the 2017 Super Bowl.

There is actually some science behind the concept of using stories in advertising; it's not just the latest flavour-of-the-month marketing angle.

When we have to process bland content, such as our business's financial accounts, the areas of the brain that activate are known as the Broca's area and the Wernicke's area, which are named after two neuroscientists who did a lot of research into this concept. In general terms, we are not hardwired to retain this type of information for any length of time. However, when we are listening to, watching or reading stories the sensory cortex is activated, and the way we relate to the story determines which sense is activated.

Our goal on LinkedIn is to move people through their journey, from the *know* phase to the *like* phase. Stories align a cause with an effect, for example, bonding an idea with an emotion. If we can achieve this on LinkedIn, the person reading our story or watching our videos has the opportunity to attach an emotion to us within themselves.

To give you an example of this, once I had made the decision to write this book based on the feedback I had received from hundreds of people, there was a process of steps that I took in the writing journey. One of those steps was the getting feedback on the cover design. Over two hundred people were kind enough to provide their thoughts on the first drafts, right through to the final version, and hopefully you will like the outcome. A number of people provided feedback, for instance: 'Having known (and enjoyed) your personality on webcasts, I don't think either of these designs bring out your personality.'

And this one: 'They are a little too complicated, which is not you. In my mind you're the uncomplicated, so the covers need to outline that.'

These kind people went as far as sharing how they would be likely to attach this book, in their thoughts, to my personality (or lack thereof). In other words, the more people that have the means to get to know us the more likely they will be to create a sense of us as we relate to them. The trick, of course, is to ensure that they relate to us in a positive way.

Keeping in mind that all of our stories are intended to elicit an emotion, of which there are many. Existing research suggests that we are capable of twenty-seven different emotions:

Admiration	Adoration	Appreciation
Amusement	Anxiety	Awe
Awkwardness	Boredom	Calmness
Confusion	Craving	Desire
Disgust	Empathy	Entrancement
Envy	Excitement	Fear
Horror	Interest	Joy
Nostalgia	Romance	Sadness
Satisfaction	Sympathy	Triumph

Clearly, we probably want to steer clear of a number of these. These are the ones we most want to create in our viewers:

Admiration	Appreciation	Amusement
Awe	Craving	Excitement
Interest	Joy	Satisfaction

There are three critical stories that you need to focus on to help people make this transition from simply knowing you to liking you, and they are your story, your clients' stories, and your business's story.

Telling these stories in a way that engenders some of these nine positive emotions is a sure-fire and proven method for allowing people the opportunity to like us in a way that resonates for them.

In personal branding, we are often told to create the persona we want people to know us for. I agree with that to a large extent, but I also believe that within the framework of that personal brand, allowing our connections and followers to attach to our brand the emotions that serve them best is one of the keys to shifting from simply having a personal brand to becoming an influencer with a personal brand.

Your story

At the beginning of this book I shared my story with you at the request of many of the people I reached out to for feedback on the type of book I was thinking of writing. It was one of those eat-your-own-dog-food moments for me.

Think about that. It means that telling our stories is the logical way to get people to like us, if for no other reason than it gives insight into who we are, and what interests or motivates them to seek us out online or in person. There are a number of ways that we can share our stories, both in the sense of how we deliver them—written word, audio files such as podcasts, videos—and in the context in which they are delivered.

I suggest that all three of these mediums are important because people tend to absorb information in preferred ways. For me, it is the written word. If I want to retain information, I will always seek the written version. My wife Julie much prefers a visual version, with images or video. Audio books are growing in popularity since many people seem to prefer these to the written word these days (more on this in a later chapter).

67

I should make it clear that I'm not talking about a one-off piece of content, whether it's a video or written version of your life story. That's one piece of the story, and an important one, for sure. I strongly encourage you to create that content piece in as much detail as you're comfortable sharing. However, the most important point is that these stories are ongoing and take a number of forms. Here is a list of different approaches to your story (we go into this in more depth in a later chapter):

- Recap
- Rant
- Journey
- Learning
- Struggle
- Defining moments

Your personal and ongoing story is your opportunity to create a real connection with people on a deeper level in the online sense. Make this a part of your journey to influence and you'll be well on your way to giving people the opportunity to like you. In so doing, you'll be opening up the possibility for them to take another step through their journey with you.

Your clients' stories

Almost as important as your own story are the stories of your clients. People reading such a story will often be able to relate to that person.

This will help your connections take the step from *like* to *trust*. It will also help to get a transition from followers to connections, which will again deepen that LinkedIn relationship. We all want followers, but we all value connections over followers.

There are two powerful ways you can use your clients' stories.

Case study of a client: Case studies show results, but they also are an amazing way to humanise your product or service (I have included a number of these throughout this book). This is the difference between a narrative that explains the features and benefits of your unique and remarkable solutions, and giving future clients or potential clients the opportunity to visualise those outcomes for themselves.

Hopefully, somewhere among your case studies will be a real person who has enough in common with a potential client for them to feel the excitement of imagining that a similar thing might just be in their future, too. I'm sure it goes without saying that you will need your client's permission to create a case study on them and share it on your website or in any other form of promotion.

A client's journey with you: The second way you can use a client's story is to write about their journey with you from your perspective. In this instance, you might not necessarily name the client you are referring to. The idea is to portray something that working together created for them, for instance, it could be a client they secured using your methodology, or an industry award they won, or any other positive outcome that was created by working together.

This could take the form of a written post you create, in which case you might not be specific as to whom the client is. Instead, you would focus on the story of the journey that was responsible for the outcome.

Another powerful option would be to interview your client and really showcase them—more so than yourself. This is best done through video or audio content, and the outcome of this story, in whatever form it takes, would be to make it relatable to other people, enabling them to make the connection between themselves and the outcome your current client was able to achieve with your help.

Your business's story

At some point people will be ready to go a little deeper in their journey as your client, and at this stage they will probably want more information about your business's story before being ready to look closely at your products and services. They will probably have already been exposed to your story, and have some sense of who you are and why you matter in their world. They have probably also seen, read or heard some client stories, and made the connection between someone else and themselves.

Getting some insight into your business, your team and what you stand for beyond profits will now be of interest to them, and it's important that they not only like you but also like what your business is about. Sharing your business's *why* is what I am referring to here, which is very different to your personal *why*. This explains why you get up every day and do what you do. Your business *why* is more about the reasons for your business's existence, the problem in the world your business is here to solve, and how the world is a better place because of it.

We have a page on our website that we refer to as the 'impact page': www.webtrafficthatworks.com/impact. Interestingly, our analytics show that it's one of the most viewed pages on our site. Our *why* is on this page and as you will see it simply states: 'At Web Traffic That Works we believe real and meaningful change comes through the world's entrepreneurs; people just like you. Our purpose is to help you create a powerful online presence that grows and accelerates your global footprint, so that together we really can make a huge impact.'

On the rest of the page we share our passion for creating important impacts in the world through our partnership with the global giving movement, B1G1. The story we regularly tell is about our driving force towards our goals for those impacts. For some time that goal was to achieve one million impacts, and I'm proud to share with you that we exceeded that goal and are now shooting for twelve million impacts as our next goal.

We share the story of how our clients are responsible for creating these impacts and how every service we offer is aligned with specific impacts that are created, such as providing food, medicines, clean drinking water, education, and many more life-changing services for people in need around the world. These stories probably create two of the most powerful emotions in people: joy and appreciation.

If you don't yet have a purpose beyond profit, now might be the time to consider what resonates with you and your team in creating your business *why*. If you'd like more information about B1G1, go to their website: www.B1G1.com. Or if you would like a personal introduction to their team just drop us an email at: clientdelight@webtrafficthatworks. com. We will be more than happy to do that for you.

Your business may already have a purpose for existing or, more importantly, a purpose beyond just profit. (Let me be really clear: I have nothing against profit. Every business has a responsibility to be profitable, and, where applicable, every business owner has a responsibility to provide a comfortable and rewarding way of life for their family.)

Either way, make sure to showcase your business's *why* in your stories, and, just like with the previous two story options, this will be an ongoing sharing of these stories. It is a journey as much as it is about a dedicated page on your website or marketing statement.

Your business's *why* doesn't have to be about charitable giving, it can be about anything you choose. There are only two critical steps you need adhere to: ensure that you have a *why*, and regularly share your *why* in your stories.

Clarity Message

Amanda Bigelow

Amanda is a food-as-medicine and personal-lifestyle practitioner. She works with high-achieving women who have come to a crossroads with their health, and she specialises in helping them to get their energy back, heal their bodies and create a healthy, productive life.

She is also the author of *Powered by Health: The High-Achieving Woman's Guide to Health, Vitality, and a New Life Full of Possibilities.*

What was the biggest challenge you were having with LinkedIn before doing the 12-Week Influencer Program?

I lacked any real knowledge about how to use LinkedIn to generate leads. I wanted to build a thriving, interesting community of business people all over the world, but had no idea of how to go about it.

How has your time on LinkedIn changed since completing the program?

I spend more time doing things that create momentum and establish me as key person of influence. I now create status posts or LinkedIn Pulse articles three times a week. I'm also generating around twenty-five new leads every week and I regularly establish new partnerships. This is my main business-development platform now.

Can you share one or two amazing benefits you have experienced since completing the program?

I have established a really interesting partnership with two women who have their own fashion label and retail shops in the US and Canada. They're expanding into products for their existing clients, including health and wellness. We have developed a simple plan for my services and products to be promoted to their elite membership of high-achieving women. I've also formed solid relationships with women in Australia, England and the USA.

How has this impacted you, either personally or as results for your business?

I have much more momentum than ever before in my business. Things are happening with more ease, I'm reaching my niche more and it's working. My business confidence has grown, and I love the way LinkedIn allows me to meet so many interesting and amazing people. Working on this platform feels right and very authentic. I consider myself a global citizen and LinkedIn helps me to be this.

Amanda Bigelow

www.linkedin.com/in/amandabigelow

www.amandabigelow.com

CHAPTER 9

Engagement the Influencer Way

ngagement. It's almost a buzzword itself in social media these days;
everyone is talking about the importance of engagement on your
content. I just did a Google search using the words 'How do I get
engagement on my social media content' and it returned 179 million
results, containing all the usual stuff:

- Make your posts visual
- Create surveys
- Add hashtags
- Run contests
- Engage on other people's content

You will also find free courses, paid courses, platforms that create so
called 'engaging content', seven ways to this, ten ways to that, the top one
hundred this, thirty-five effective that, and much more.

Some of this information is helpful and some not so much. Now,
don't get me wrong, I'm not trying to downplay the importance of having
engaging content (in the next chapter this is covered very specifically as

it relates to creating influence). It's just not the type of engagement I'm referring to as one of the nine drivers of influence.

The type of engagement I'm talking about is the type that almost nobody who perceives themselves as social-media influencers creates (see chapter two for the difference between 'influencers' and 'influential'), which is to engage with the comments or points of view that people leave on your content.

Responding to followers

I was listening to a talkback radio show in my car on the way to the beach yesterday, and one of the show hosts referred to a celebrity who actually responds to many of the comments left by his fans on his social-media profiles. The host seemed to be in awe of the fact that he did this, and pointed out how rare it is for celebrities to engage in the way this person did, and how it set him apart.

One level down from celebrities are the influencers, who may just be well known on one particular platform such as YouTube or Instagram, and are generating income and or free products through their profiles. More often than not, these people rarely engage with those who are giving them the opportunity to have their piece of fame. When you go onto their profiles and their content, what you see are one-sided interactions. In fairness to some, the amount of commentary required is often huge and it would be difficult for them to reply to every comment; many of the better-paid ones employ people to respond as them on their behalf.

My point here is that our type of influencer *does* respond to the comments left by people on their content on LinkedIn, and to the direct messages that people send (with the exception of the spam content, of course). This is by far one of the major differences that set these influencers apart, placing them in the previously mentioned 0.02 percent of people on LinkedIn.

The reality is that you're not talking about or realistically attempting to have thousands of comments on your content. You are niching in fields of expertise, and therefore appealing to a laser-focused group of people, not the masses of a celebrity endorsement or general social media.

Yes, I have had, and many of my clients have had, individual pieces of content generate hundreds of thousands of views on our content and profiles, plus thousands of likes and comments. For me personally, my most successful content piece generated in excess of five hundred thousand views, more than two thousand comments and seventy-five thousand searches on my profile in one week. These are the exceptions and not the rule, and sometimes this is what we are actively attempting to achieve. However, in the normal course of any given content piece's lifespan, it will generate views in the thousands, or occasionally ten thousand plus. Twenty to one hundred comments per post is ideal, with anything above that a welcome bonus. At these levels it's possible and realistic to respond to the people who have taken the time to engage on our content.

So, in very simple terms 'engagement' as a driver of influence is how *you* engage with people, more so than the standard definition of engagement in general social-media terms. If you're not prepared to interact with people on your content, and in the more private realm of direct messages, you will struggle to position yourself as the go-to person in your industry.

Is it okay to have your team respond as you? Yes, although I personally attempt to respond in the public face of engagement on my content. In ninety percent of occasions it will be me responding, allowing for the fact that I am often on planes, in different time zones around the world, or speaking at live events. On these occasions I don't change the timing of my content, and in fact I stick to a quite regimented posting schedule (this is covered in the next chapter). At times like this, one of my team will respond on my behalf.

The same goes for direct messages. I do this as often as possible myself, and the team keeps the momentum and response times within our guidelines when I cannot. Since I know when my content is being shared in advance, I do make time in my schedule each day for this task; I consider this one of the most important tasks I do every day.

Do some people I know fully outsource this? Yes, they do. Do they still achieve great results? Yes, they do, but only after briefing their teams extremely well on how to go about this.

How you structure this task to fit within your daily schedule is entirely up to you, although I suggest that if it's possible you do most of it personally. This will give you the best long-term results.

How you or your team respond is also a big driver of your personal brand, which we touched on previously. This is likely to be the most public, potentially scrutinised, and at times criticised part of your journey to influence.

Handling negative feedback

Many people I have coached through our 12-Week Influencer Program have gone along for months getting great traction with their content, following best practice, and then receive that inevitable piece of negative feedback, either about their point of view on a post or, more importantly, on a response they have made to someone else, who has then commented on their content. Suddenly it seems as though their world has been shattered; someone does not agree, and is quite vocal in their opinion of the subject matter.

Personally, I would celebrate this event if I were you. Ninety-nine percent of the time it will not be the end of the world as you know it. You won't need to move to a deserted island to let the dust settle. What it does mean is that you have started to become known for your point of view on your topic of expertise, and have discovered that not everyone agrees with you. This will be covered in more depth in a later chapter, but for now I will simply say that you should accept that you will get opposing opinions.

You will also get competitors looking to ride your coat tails of increasing influence, and on some occasions you will attract the haters. In Australia we use the term 'tall poppy syndrome' to describe the tendency to discredit or disparage someone else who has achieved wealth or prominence in public life. While this term is generally aimed at people in public office, or who have high status in business circles, or celebrities, it's also commonly used in all forms of social media. Social media gives the haters a public forum to do what they do. The haters are best ignored; they will move on soon enough.

How you handle the people who have a legitimately different point of view, or call you out when you make a mistake, is again what puts you in our 0.02-percent club. You should respond with complete honesty. If you firmly believe in your point of view—and you should, or you shouldn't have shared it in the first place—then justify your opinion. If you feel that the other person's point of view has some validity, acknowledge that fact.

Sometimes other people in my field don't agree with some aspects of my personal opinions on certain topics. I realise this, so when I express these opinions I will often add a caveat such as: 'This is my personal belief; however, I acknowledge that there are other credible experts in this field who do not agree.'

A simple statement like this, if you know there's a possibility of differing opinions will negate a high number of challenges to your point of view. It will also give you the ability to respond by agreeing that there can be more than one opinion on the subject matter.

If you find yourself dealing with somebody who chooses to disagree, you can agree to disagree, or you can further validate your opinion with more insights based on your experience. Engaging in debate on a subject you raise is one of the best outcomes you can achieve, and is one of the best opportunities you will be gifted for deepening your influence. However, my caveat to that is: 'As long as you can back it up.'

Dealing with competitors

When it comes to dealing with competitors, well, this is one of those topics where many people with expert opinions may not agree with me.

This is my personal belief and I acknowledge that other credible experts in this field may not agree with me.

I believe there is an abundance of everything we desire or need in this world. I am also a believer in the process I'm sharing here, and its power to set you apart from the majority of your competitors. Their attempt to ride your coat tails is flattering. If you agree, then there is nothing you need to do differently. If you don't agree and would like a strategy to ensure this does not happen, here it is.

Make a list of people you believe are competitors, or people you would not want engaging on your content. It doesn't matter if you're connected or not on LinkedIn right now. Go to their profile on LinkedIn and click on the More tab, which is in the section above the Summary. One of the options in the drop-down menu is Report/Block. Select Block. If you are first-degree connections, LinkedIn will remove them as such and prevent them from viewing your profile or your connections. It will also remove their ability to see or engage on your content. Problem solved.

As your influence increases, so too, potentially, will you find more people you want to add to this blocked status, so just block them as and when you see fit. Definitely use this strategy for bona fide haters when you encounter them.

To sum up, the engagement you have with your followers, and those who respond to your content, is the holy grail of engagement in your journey of influence. Yes, of course you want and need the standard definitions of engagement, but it's how you respond in all situations—the different opinions and the haters—that will set you above the pack. You will be unlikely to maintain a position as an influential person in your industry if you're not willing to engage in this manner.

Clarity Message

David Blair

David is a digital customer-experience specialist based in New Zealand. He helps small to medium enterprises deliver excellent online customer experiences to their prospects and clients, allowing them to accelerate sales and gain customers for life.

What was the biggest challenge you were having with LinkedIn before doing the 12-Week Influencer Program?

My biggest challenge was how to go about marketing myself online. I'd tried a number of other paid programs that didn't fit with my values of transparency, openness, and honesty. I didn't see LinkedIn as something I could use effectively for networking or business. It was just another social-media platform.

How has your time spent on LinkedIn changed since completing the program?

Now I spend more time creating my own content than reading the content of others. I also spend more time on LinkedIn overall because I'm getting great interaction and building really good online relationships, a number of which have now developed to include face-to-face business.

Can you share one or two amazing benefits you have experienced since completing the program?

In the last month of the program I had two speaking engagements directly from new LinkedIn contacts, with follow-up workshop requests. At the start of the program I had just over five hundred connections, which quickly grew to over one thousand, and they are exactly the right type of people I need to be connecting with.

I used to get around 150 views on most of my posts. Now I get around 1,500 on average, with one post receiving over eight thousand. My average views still continue to climb. I can see much greater value in the future time I will be spending on LinkedIn, too.

How has this impacted you, either personally or as results for your business?

Early on in the program, Adam pointed out that my messaging and what I want to be known for was too confusing and didn't present clear value to anyone. This caused me to take stock and seek help. I now have much clearer messaging, and am on the track to develop a truly unique selling position across all of my online profiles and materials.

David Blair

www.linkedin.com/in/david-blair-nz

https://david.co.nz

CHAPTER 10

The Content Plan

'Stop writing about everything. So many brands
create content and try to cover everything,
instead of focusing on the core niche that they
can position themselves as an expert around.
No one cares about your special recipe ... Find
your niche, and then go even more niche.'

—Joe Pulizzi

If engagement was not a big eye-opener for you, then content probably will be. In fact, it could be argued that this chapter should have preceded engagement, given that my definition of engagement relates mostly to your content. I'm reminded right now of that question, 'Which came first, the chicken or the egg?' To me it doesn't matter because I love chicken and eggs equally, and it's a similar distinction here as to which should come first. My reason for putting engagement first is so you have a deeper understanding of the need to create content, and why the type of content created is so important.

Either way, strap in and grab your notebook if you haven't already. This is the longest chapter of this book. If you've been powering through and are close to needing a break, take it now and come back when you're refreshed.

This chapter highlights where the majority of people go wrong on LinkedIn, in general and also on the journey to becoming highly influential. Sharing the wrong content can destroy your personal brand in a similar way to engaging with your community, so before we dive into an effective content strategy, let's start with my five guidelines for things to be aware of and possibly avoid.

1. **LinkedIn is not Facebook or Instagram.** You are looking to create a personal brand using LinkedIn as your chosen platform. It is not the place to share your social life and the latest things going on with your family and friends. There's nothing wrong with doing that, but it's not appropriate to do it on LinkedIn. If you want to know about those kinds of things going on in my world, by all means connect with me on Facebook or Instagram. You're very welcome to see that side of my life. Even our cat has his own Instagram page, with a few thousand followers; he gets more love on there than I do. Just look for CrazyCatCharli.

2. **Too much content.** Influence is not generated through quantity of content; it comes through quality content. You don't need to treat your LinkedIn profile like Twitter and share content every hour of the day. The more content you share on LinkedIn, the less likely you will be to gain traction. This is due to the way the algorithms deal with

content shown in feeds, and the suppression of what is deemed low quality tactics, or spam content.

3. **Spamming groups.** I've seen so many so-called LinkedIn strategies that suggest you should join as many groups as possible (you can join one hundred in total), and push out as many links to your blog posts and latest offers that you can. On the flip side, I see many people complaining that groups on LinkedIn don't get anywhere near the traction that other platforms achieve. Ask yourself if you really want to spend your precious time looking over endless pitches by group members. Or is your reason for choosing to join a group more about community, and a place to learn and interact with other like-minded people? Influential people are active in groups; they are not active in this manner.

4. **Self-promotion.** By all means promote yourself and what it is you do, but be aware that there is an acceptable limit on how much you do this. You will soon encounter my 13-point content plan, but here's a heads-up. Only two out of every thirteen pieces of content will be self-promotional.

Think of the last party or networking event you attended. Who was the person everyone talked about but did not enjoy talking to? It was probably the person who never stopped talking about themselves. In real life we don't warm to people who do this, and we don't tolerate it online either. As you become more influential, more and more people will want to know your story and what you have to say; they just don't want every piece of content you share to be about you.

5. **Curated content.** You'll recall that I stated previously that there are times when I will share my point of view and add the caveat explaining that it's my personal belief and I acknowledge that there are other credible experts in this field who do not agree with me. Well, this is another personal point of view.

I see lots of strategies suggesting that creating influence is simple. All you need to do is find articles written by other experts and share them with your community, suggesting that, in your opinion, it's worth their taking the time to read them. You might think this is a more effective strategy than taking the time to create your own quality content. I respectfully disagree. In my opinion, it's far better to be the person others refer to, and whose content and opinions others share.

I'm not suggesting that there isn't a place for sharing other people's content (you'll see where this fits into our 13-point content plan very soon), but I do question the wisdom of an entire strategy revolving around curated content.

From here on in the book I will use the word 'community' a great deal; in fact, the very next chapter is dedicated to the individuals that make up your community. These are the people who believe what you believe: they follow you or connect with you, and most importantly they regularly engage with your content (more about these very special people in the next chapter).

Now that you know what you *shouldn't* being doing, it's time to get clear on what you *should* be doing as it relates to your content strategy. There are four steps for you to implement.

Step 1: The right content

Just as there are five things you should not do in your content strategy, equally there are five content types you should focus on:

1. Text-only status updates: These posts, which will show up in your connections and followers feeds, are short-form bite-sized pieces of content. Although they are short in word count, they can pack a big punch. They often have the ability to create the most engagement when you share your expertise regularly. Keep in mind that more and more people are consuming content via their phones these days, so short-form content that is well written and targeted to your niche is likely to be favourably received by your community.

2. Text with images: These are the same as your text-only posts, with the addition of an image or images. If you were writing a blog post or creating a new web page, you would likely spend a lot of time and energy on making sure you add the right images. Interestingly, I find that content with images gets less traction on LinkedIn than just text-based content. My tips regarding image selection are to keep it relevant to the subject matter, and also avoid the overuse of stock images. Screenshots or real-life images often seem to work best.

3. Native video: Video has the potential to be the holy grail of content; however, on LinkedIn there are a few guidelines to follow to get the best traction for your videos:

    *   Videos should always be 'native upload', which means that you upload the video file directly onto the platform, either via your

desktop or your phone. Avoid using YouTube or Vimeo links; videos loaded directly into LinkedIn will always get better reach than links to other platforms.

- Videos should be kept to around two minutes in length. If it runs beyond this people will be much less likely to watch it, or at least watch it to the end. Just like your short-form, text-based status-update posts, videos are usually watched on phones, and the better you are at creating punchy information-rich content the more likely you are to attract your community.

- Captions are a must; most video content—in fact, over eighty-five percent—is watched without sound. This is not specific to LinkedIn, but it is as relevant to LinkedIn as it is to all other platforms. It does take a lot more effort to create video content with captions, but if you don't use them the majority of your videos, and the message they contain, will be missed.

4. Curated content: Yes, there is a place for this type of content in your strategy, but it is well below the above three content types in importance so use it sparingly. When appropriate, ensure that you tag the author into your post on LinkedIn and give your opinion as to why you believe this is content worth reading for your community. I believe that the best-curated content you can use is that which already exists on LinkedIn; you can simply share a status post, native video or article that your chosen author has already uploaded recently. Sharing external links to any form of content, such as blog articles, YouTube Videos and landing pages, is something that tends to be suppressed in feeds.

As your feeds get busier, LinkedIn will attempt to keep what you see on the platform itself. I believe that more social platforms will take this approach in the future, which is why curated content is having less traction as a strategy in itself. It does and will have relevance, however, if you only share relevant posts that don't use external links, and were authored directly on LinkedIn.

5. Articles: LinkedIn gives you your own blogging platform as part of your personal profile. In years gone by this was where they placed most of the emphasis—on sharing content into feeds—and this is why you can see over one hundred and fifty articles I have published on LinkedIn. These days the short-form status post rules, reinforcing the move towards consuming content on mobile devices.

This doesn't mean that you shouldn't use this type of longer-form content at times. One of the values of articles is that they stay anchored to your profile. When someone chooses to take a close look at your profile page, your most recent article is right there on show. You can double down on the value of the articles by sharing a status post linking to your article into the future.

Step 2: The content plan

We have used this exact framework—the 13-point content plan—with over three hundred clients with great success, and I'm going to make it really simple for you to create your own content plan. If you follow this advice exactly, your content will be compliant with LinkedIn's preferences;

you will have the perfect amount of content without overdoing it and having some of your content suppressed. And you will have an easy process that is easy to replicate and follow month after month.

I suggest you include the following in your monthly content plan:

- Long-form article
- Curated article
- Status posts with images
- Native videos
- Status posts with no images

These posts should be a mixture of content that your community would want to consume and content that positions you as highly influential in your industry without seeming too 'salesy'. I recommend that you divide the posts into four categories:

1. Interesting: Your stories will cross all categories. Hopefully it's obvious that your stories could easily fall into the interesting category; however, they are not the only type of content that does. Those in your community will also have opinions, so one of the most interesting content pieces could be where you start the conversation and allow your community, through the comments, to share theirs. Of course, this will vary immensely from industry to industry, and possibly country to country.

    Here is an example of a status post I shared that had over fifteen thousand views and eighty points of view shared:

Congrats on the promotion! Congrats on the promotion! Congrats on the promotion! You may as well be a robot if you send default messages like this … I set up a new role on my LinkedIn profile as founder of our 12-Week Influencer Program, then promptly got over 300 identical messages. But a small group of 20 or so people had taken the time to send a genuine, personalised message. They brought a smile to my face.

I can appreciate the intention of someone who sends a quick, pre-typed message. But honestly, to me it comes across as low effort, and thus a low intention to really mean anything. It's the same as connecting with someone. If you think you'll value the connection, take the time to write a personalised message. Delivering the standard message is saying that you're too lazy to write a proper note, and don't really value connecting in the first place.

What do you think of the automated replies LinkedIn is giving us access to? Do you love them or hate them?

I posed a point of view and allowed my community to weigh in with their thoughts as well; this created the engagement I referred to in the last chapter and gave my community a voice to be heard.

2. Industry: Your content should also be about your industry; you need to show that you're at the cutting edge of your field of expertise. If there's breaking news or some form of change in the status quo, by forming an opinion or simplifying the complicated you're showing that you care enough to keep your community updated, or making what is likely common knowledge easier to understand.

While you will need to create your status posts or videos, there will be a plethora of industry bodies, podcasts, groups or news articles about every facet of your industry. All you need to do is subscribe to any of your preferred options and your content will almost create itself, which means that you need to do very little research into the subject matter. The key is to have an opinion for or against, and phrase it as a question so your community can share their opinions, too. The topic might be well known, but you are now the industry expert because you asked the question.

I'll use another post of mine as an example:

It feels like a lot of my LinkedIn connections are speakers. But did you know glossophobia, or fear of public speaking, is so widely feared that it's considered a worse fate than death?!

I also love delivering keynotes. But it is a funny realisation that we speakers are in fact the outliers, that the world at large, outside my tiny world, is really afraid of speaking.

It seems I've unwittingly become part of a 'speaker bubble', where a lot of my connections like to speak, and so I see more and more of it. So now I'm trying to pop it, not only to keep me sane, but also to see if there are any LinkedIn users who are comfortable saying they don't get fired up by the opportunity to speak.

So tell me, what's your view on speaking? Does it petrify you, or do you live for the stage?

Short and to the point—just eight sentences in total—but it packed a punch for plenty of people who had an opinion to share.

3. Promotional: Of course, we all want to be able to promote our events, services, special offers, etc. There's no point in being active on social media if it doesn't lead to revenue generation of some description. So, yes, you can and should create promotional content, but it should only be to promote that next step we have spoken about. In my opinion this is a rookie mistake I see daily on LinkedIn: in most cases people go in for the kill, so to speak, too early.

When it's appropriate to create this type of content, make sure you have built your funnel, and create your promotional content to move people to the next step in their buyer's journey. As we have already discussed, this could be to come to your webinar, or your free event, or to have an online meeting where you will be providing some great value.

I have only used written posts as examples in this section; these posts can, and at times should be, video content. To view an example where I used both written and video content, go to www.linkedin.com/feed/update/urn:li:activity:6430906574319034368.

This was the written content that accompanies that video:

[FREE GIFT]

I've been applying the Key Person of Influence methodology for a few years now and seen amazing results, so I've teamed up with them to offer you a couple free gifts!

They have a proven 5-step process that just works.

They've helped hundreds of businesses stand out and scale up, and they've donated more than $4 million dollars through charitable giving.

So I reached out to Michael Clark (Dent's State Leader for Queensland) and asked if there's anything we could do to pass on some value to you.

We've come up with two free gifts:

The Influence Score Card This free 40-question test benchmarks your ability to influence in a business or leadership context and identifies opportunities for leveraged growth.

And The Key Person of Influence book shows you how to use the 5Ps methodology to become more visible, valuable, and connected in your industry.

Grab them from the links below (no strings attached)

I'm sure you're thinking, that's great, Adam, but how does it help me? A promotion like this has the potential to be very powerful on many levels. Still using the same example, let me outline a few of the advantages for me from this connection:

- I am now in the position of being highly influential; I have partnered with a world-class business Dent (www.dent.global).
- My community receives valuable and free content through Dent's scorecard and book, and the best part is that I didn't have to create any of the content (other than the post and video).
- Dent will reciprocate the favour by promoting something of mine at a later date that is also free.
- Both Dent and I benefit because the suggestion to take up the free offer is by someone else rather than ourselves, and we both get to expose in an appropriate way our first step in our funnels to a new audience. We've added value to our respective communities to mutual benefit.

You can do the standard promotion where you simply offer your own next step in the funnel, a concept that I'm sure doesn't require any in-depth explanation.

4. The rant: Ah, the rant, one of my favourite content strategies. If there's anything that gets the opinions flowing it's a good rant. I'm sure you're all familiar with the rant. Briefly, it's a tirade or venting of frustration. It's you on your soapbox telling the world you're sick of seeing something occur. A word of warning: use the rant sparingly or you risk being seen as a whinger. You might get a few comments to this effect on each post, and for now just take my word for it that this is quite okay (I will explain why in more detail in the next chapter).

In my opinion, the best way of using a rant is to combine it with a promotional objective, although it's more than acceptable to just simply allow your community their voice. The key is not just to rant but to also offer a solution. This will move you from being a potential whinger to the person with the answers: the industry influencer, if you like.

Here is my favourite one of all time: *If you want my best advice, close your LinkedIn account today!* Harsh words, but it was the best advice I could give. Let me share the backstory.

Someone contacted me asking for my advice on how to use LinkedIn to reach out to and sell to as many people as possible. He started the conversation by saying, 'I don't want to spend all day on LinkedIn connecting with people. I don't have time to be writing articles or answering people's questions. And I don't want to have conversations with people off LinkedIn either.'

I responded by asking him, 'What exactly *do* you want'?'

'I just want to be able to direct people to our landing pages,' he said, 'so that hopefully they will buy our courses.'

Hence my rather harsh response to him to close his LinkedIn account.

It's not that difficult to generate plenty of business through LinkedIn, but there are some fundamental issues that you need to be aware of. If you would like some tips on best practice for LinkedIn marketing, reply in the comments. If you're in Australia, I'll send you a copy of my book *The LinkedIn Playbook* (copies limited to the first twenty people who respond). If you're outside Australia, I will send you the PDF version. There's no opt-in required, and no, I won't add you to any database. Consider it a New Year's gift with no strings attached.

Step 3: The content mix

Hopefully, by now you have some great content ideas, and an understanding of the right type of content. Here's my suggestion as to how this should be broken up over any given month. It's entirely up to you what will be in video form or text-based content:

- Interesting: Seven in total that are interesting enough for your community to want to engage and get in on the conversation.

As this will represent over half of your monthly content, it makes sense, I hope, to mix it up between video, text only, and text with image.

- Your industry: Two per month that are specific to your industry, following the above format and spread a couple of weeks apart.
- Promotional: Two per month, and it's up to you to decide whether they should be spread over the month or close together. Which option is better will depend on your strategy.
- Curated: One per month, sharing someone else's content. However, if you're struggling to come up with something from each of the other four options, by all means add an extra one of these until you can build up to the full thirteen per month.
- Rant: One per month is always the maximum. As with the curated option, feel free to reduce this to every second month if you're more comfortable with that, especially in the early stages of your content creation.

Again, let me be clear here. This is what I personally consider an ideal mix and amount of content. If you're new to content creation and this seems a daunting task, start with a lower number. Many people in our 12-Week Influencer Program choose to start with four per month in the first month, and build upwards until they reach full speed and are confident they can be consistent.

I suggest it's better to start low and build than go up and down each month. Your community will get used to your level of content delivery, and consistency beats erratic every time.

Step 4: The content schedule

Based on the 13-point content plan, and being at this level consistently, you should aim to post every Monday, Wednesday and Friday, between 8.30 am and 9.00 am in the time zone where the majority of your community resides. If you're a location-based business or service provider this should be easy.

If your clients and community are all over the world, like mine, it could be more challenging. I always err on the side of simplicity. I believe that consistency is the key to long-term success. If your content follows the above process, and is relevant to your microniche, the right people will gravitate to you and your content regardless of the time zone.

We've now covered, in depth, the three drivers of the *like* phase. I'm sure it's obvious that the three stages—*know, like, trust*—are designed to build on each other, and each takes a bit more buy-in from your followers.

Getting known will be easy if you follow the process and the three drivers. Getting liked will take some work, but it's well worth the process. Creating trust is the step that will bring it all home seamlessly; and is the main driver of effortless sales. They must follow each other in a logical sequence, however, to be effective. Take all the time you need in the *like* phase before moving onto *trust*. And then when you're ready, move onto the next section.

Clarity Message

Tracy Sheen

Tracy helps associations increase their membership; she is also the founder of Unusual Comms, a podcaster and author, and now hosts LinkedIn local events in Brisbane, Australia.

Unusual Comms is an agency devoted to a methodology that is a clever way of engaging with clients, team members, suppliers and the broader community, using technology to help give people back their time. From website copy to social media, newsletters to articles, webinars to podcasts, the agency takes a 360-degree look at a business and ensures that the messaging is cutting through the fog and relating to people in a way that suits the intended audience.

What was the biggest challenge you were having with LinkedIn before doing the 12-Week Influencer Program?

Visibility. I had a profile, but no engagement, or leads being generated from being on LinkedIn.

How has your time spent on LinkedIn changed since completing the program?

I now have direction on building a LinkedIn sales funnel, and the engagement I'm creating is increasing my visibility week by week.

Can you share one or two amazing benefits you have experienced since completing the program?

On #jeansforgenes day I posted about the day: what I actually thought was an innocuous little post. I was contacted and connected with the head of fundraising for the organisation. I'm now in discussions with them about creating content.

How has this impacted you, either personally or as results for your business?

It's opened up the associations space for me to promote and connect with influencers that I hadn't previously considered. I have far more conversations happening now than I would have ever considered possible, and a percentage of those will filter through to become clients.

Tracy Sheen

www.linkedin.com/in/tracysheen

www.unusualcomms.com.au

CHAPTER 11

Community and How to Build Yours

'Where there is not community, trust, respect,
ethical behaviour are difficult for the young
to learn and for the old to maintain.'
—Robert K Greenleaf

Let me ask you a question. When was the last time you made a significant purchase from someone you didn't trust? Unless you're selling Lamborghinis for $1,995 (and even then, most people would think twice) if people don't trust you it's a hard slog to turn them into clients.

Creating that trust is a much easier road if people already know who you are, have a clear understanding of what you do, and they like you. And as I have outlined, there are three drivers of trust: building a community, becoming a problem solver, and creating advocates.

So, let's dive right into the process of building a community, but before we do that let me explain why it matters.

Nobody wants to go first. Have you ever been to an auction for a house in a slow real-estate market, or given a presentation where you've asked the audience for input? Nobody wants to go first. But as soon as someone kicks off the bidding, or has given the first response, everything starts to flow.

It's the same with clients. Nobody wants to be your first client, and regardless of how long you've been doing what you do, every new client will be nervously deciding whether or not they want to take that leap of faith in you.

You can build trust one client at a time, and every time, or you can build a community of people who believe what you believe, are happy to be a part of your community, and sing your praises. People will feel reassured to know you have a community in place, and they can see a constant stream of activity from and to you, and an engaged tribe of people who seem to be just like them, by which I mean that they are interested in you, your expertise, and in working with you.

Community = Trust

Once people know you have your own community, trust will be established in most cases *before* you get to the sales conversation instead of it *being* the sales conversation. Think back over any recent interactions you've had that didn't end up with that person getting to the sales-conversation step. To those people actively looking for someone to solve their particular problem, you are a potential candidate. Maybe they've been to your website, and they've been following you for a while on LinkedIn and are seeing your content regularly.

When someone takes the first step from being a content consumer to being a potential client, the most important hurdle for them to overcome is finding out if they can trust you to solve their problem. This is where the conversation starts. If you cannot convince them of your trustworthiness, the conversation will go no further. They will go looking for alternatives, someone else to talk to.

Now imagine if they could become immersed in your community of like-minded people. That conversation would be much more likely to be about your service rather than whether you're the right person for them. As the leader of the community, your ability to influence and be seen as an influencer will be exponentially higher than if you simply remain the content creator for other people to use to establish influence.

Having a great book on a subject, or creating regular high-quality content, will lift you above the masses in influence; having your own community will up your game every time.

Meet-ups

Every community needs a home, a place to gather and share their thoughts, ask their questions, and interact with each other. If your clients tend to be localised in the same region, you might want to meet with your tribe face to face through regular meet-ups. You can use the Meetup website (www.meetup.com) as the home of your new community. You can use the functional site to set up your own group within minutes. Given that millions of people across the globe know, like and trust the website Meetup, it would be my platform of choice to use.

The real magic, though, happens through the live format of your group. There is simply no better way to build a community than having the ability to meet face to face on a regular basis. It allows your tribe to bring their colleagues and friends along, too, multiplying your community for you.

In most cases your community is best built online. No matter which one you choose, the objective should be clear and there should be rules to abide by. Make sure both of these are clearly stated and followed by you and your community members. There are three options to choose from.

1. **LinkedIn group.** Given that you're building your influence on LinkedIn, it makes sense for you to create your group on LinkedIn, too, since it's the easy option for keeping everything in one place. This is probably where the majority of people will build theirs.

2. **Facebook group.** Facebook, in my opinion, does groups better than any other online platform. This is where mine is located and you are very welcome to join us at www.facebook.com/groups/LinkedIn2Success.

Given that our group is one hundred percent about LinkedIn, it might seem a little odd that I have created the group on Facebook. If any group should be on LinkedIn, mine would fit that bill. I have two specific reasons for using Facebook.

The first is to spread risk. A reality we should all be mindful of is that we do not own any of our online profiles; most of us simply have rent-free access, and in some cases not even that. LinkedIn owns your LinkedIn profile, Facebook owns your Facebook profile, and the same can be said for every other social-media platform in existence today.

These organisations all change their rules regularly. I could share stories with you of businesses I know of that built their entire marketing ecosystem around both LinkedIn and Facebook, only to have their accounts closed on them for seemingly minor infringements of the rules. So I choose not to have all of my eggs in the one LinkedIn basket.

My second reason for using Facebook is that, as already stated, I believe Facebook groups are far superior to LinkedIn groups with regard to user friendliness.

3. **Membership site.** There is no shortage of options when it comes to platforms you can use to custom-build your own community site. These include Wordpress, Ontraport, Memberpress, SubHub, Wild Apricot, Wishlist, Membergate, Memberful, to name just a few. Building your own platform will require a lot more time to set up, and there will likely be an associated cost as well. One of these websites will, however, give you the ability to design things exactly the way you want them to be.

   It doesn't matter where you build your community, only that you have one and that you are the founder of it. Once you've established your community, it should be included in your title on your LinkedIn profile. I also suggest that you create a position description that outlines what your group is all about, with a link to the group—this is one of those game-changing tactics that will make you stand out above the pack.

   I should point out not all of your clients will want to be a member of your online community. Some will prefer to keep to themselves and just want you as their chosen service provider. They will still be swayed by your influence as the founder, however, so it's essential that they can easily see that your group exists. So make it obvious in your title, and give it its own position description on your LinkedIn profile.

Having your own group is impressive in itself, but it's what you do with your group that makes all the difference. The majority of groups I see don't create influence for their founders. Rather, they are ghost towns of sorts. They may have impressive follower counts, but if nobody is active in the group it's doing more harm than good.

Of course, the most active person in your group should be you. If you're not visiting your group daily, or at least Monday to Friday, as well as creating conversations and nurturing your community, you will miss the biggest value proposition your group offers.

There is a plethora of groups that attempt to create a real sense of community but follow a tired methodology of having themed days. Mentor Monday, Wednesday Wins, Friday Funnies and the like. These groups are at least trying to be engaging, but in my opinion these strategies fall short because they rely on the community to be posting and engaging.

A better strategy for you is to be the one posting and starting the conversations. There is nothing wrong with following a set routine that your group members get used to.

Q&A sessions

One of the best ways to generate high engagement is to hold regular Q&A sessions where your group members can send in questions about your chosen area of expertise. In answering them, you have a great opportunity to expand beyond your microniche and showcase your wider expertise, if that is appropriate for you.

These Q&A sessions can be done in two different ways. The first option is to simply pose the question yourself. An example from our group is where I might pose a question like: *Would you prefer your LinkedIn profile to generate leads or position you as credible?*

The second option is to hold a live Q&A session. If you're using Facebook, you can do this through Facebook Live, which is only visible to your members. Or you can invite your members to a live webinar that you run regularly. I like Zoom as a webinar platform, but there are plenty of other good options, too. You can then answer the questions your community has and upload the recorded session for those who couldn't make the live session to watch later if they choose to.

Managing your group

The number of your followers is not the most important factor, but you should be actively looking to grow your group. One of the best ways to do this is to invite your new and existing LinkedIn connections to come and see what it's all about, provided the people you invite would be likely to gain some value from being a part of your community.

I suggest you have two strategies for this step. The first is simply to go through your current connections and make a list of those whom you would believe would benefit from membership. Give them a bit of an outline of what they should expect from their free membership and invite them to join.

The second option is to invite all of your new connections going forward, regardless of whether they request to connect with you or vice versa. Be proactive. Inviting them to check it out after you have connected is a great way to start a conversation, and it will also provide free value without making you look pushy.

I suggest that you don't start your group before the previous six drivers we have covered are underway. What comes first is having a great profile, and a clear message about what your superpower is, and honing that down to your microniche. Give people the opportunity to decide they like you through your stories, by seeing that you're responsive to their engagement, and of course by creating that amazing content. This is important to get underway because people who know and like you are far more likely to want to join your community.

My final piece of advice before we move onto the next driver is to ensure that you have the ability to moderate your community's ability to post to your group. Allowing off-topic content to roam inside your group will only annoy your members, especially if, as it often does, it revolves around members pitching their services to your members.

All good platforms will give you the option to moderate posts before they are visible to your members. If you have a repeat offender, you can privately message them and politely remind them of your objectives and rules. If they continue then it's time to remove them altogether.

Clarity Message

Sean Gordon

Sean is CEO and founder of SchoolAid, a charitable organisation 'empowering young philanthropists'. Sean is also a business coach best known as 'the growth mindset coach'. He helps people, and organisations, that are stuck by exploring the conditioning that causes them to behave the way they do, even when they know better. He delivers proven strategies to quickly and effectively change paradigms that are not serving them well by addressing the causes rather than the symptoms, which include poor thinking, bad habits, and limiting beliefs. He is a keynote speaker, and is passionate about living clean and giving people the best possible opportunities to thrive.

This is what Sean had to say after his 90-day journey through the influencer program.

What was the biggest challenge you were having with LinkedIn before doing the 12-Week Influencer Program?
Describing what I do and being clear on the people I was really seeking as my ideal clients. I wasn't getting any meaningful cut-through on LinkedIn.

How has your time spent on LinkedIn changed since completing the program?
It has completely changed. I'm there every day now, but with a focus on productive activities like posting quality content regularly, responding, inviting, helping others with their scene, and growing my network.

Can you share one or two amazing benefits you have experienced since completing the program?

My posts are being viewed in increasing numbers, and I know from comments that I'm becoming a 'thought leader' in my space. The methodology you created for us has opened my eyes to other possibilities, and my involvement has been both educational and productive. People who don't comment online tell me they see my posts, and a couple have come forward to explore my offering. It's amazing how many people are watching what I'm doing but choosing not to comment publicly. I'm gaining new clients with this program and my presence is part of the conversion.

How has this impacted you, either personally or as results for your business?

I'm a better product of my own (and your) advice, and I worry less about being perfect. Instead, I get on and do the thing. I have met some terrific people in our group, and in some cases we have connected outside of that to add further value for each other.

Sean Gordon

www.linkedin.com/in/sean-gordon-for-results

www.seangordon.com.au

www.schoolaidtrust.com

CHAPTER 12

Problem Solving

'It's so much easier to suggest solutions when
you don't know too much about the problem.'
—Malcolm Forbes

Everyone has a problem they need solved, and everyone loves the person who can solve it for them. Being very clear about the problem you solve is the fundamental backbone of your reason for becoming an influencer in your industry. It's the thing you are known for. As we covered in earlier chapters, it should be clearly outlined in your summary and your message to market.

There are two very important ways to go about problem solving in the influencer framework. There are also a couple of problems I see constantly with the next step, so I will cover those for you here, too.

The first is of course through your unique and remarkable solution; it's your expertise in what you do, the reason people are going to reach out to you and pay you handsomely for your skill.

At this point I'm going to make the assumption that you're great at what you do. I'm sure it goes without saying that it would be extremely difficult for you to be highly influential in your industry if you are not. If you cannot put your hand on your heart and say with integrity that you are proud of your hard-earned skill and expertise, your time might be best spent on getting yourself to a point where you can do this. Then come back to this process.

Let's move onto the second way you can use problem solving in your strategy to build trust. Now that you have started building your community, you have a forum for sharing your expertise to add real value to that community. You should invite your tribe to share their questions in your community that you will provide solutions for.

I can hear that question forming in your mind right now: *If I share all of my expertise for free, why would anyone need to pay me for my advice?*

I've lost count of how many times I have had this conversation. Let me assure you that the more you share your expertise, the more trust you will create and the more trust your community will have in you, beyond the enquiries you will have for your paid solutions. A lot of the content you share is going to solve problems for people. It's the reason they were attracted to you in the first place, and it will generate thousands of positive comments into the future.

The next chapter will cover this in detail, but let me just mention it quickly here. You will only have achieved influencer status when other people say you have, not when *you* do. Here's a comment left on one of my recent posts: *Your tips are priceless, Adam Houlahan ... other LinkedIn 'experts' can only eat your dust.*

Another person connected with me in this same post to find out more about our services and she is now a client. When we first spoke together on a Zoom call, she shared with me her reason for contacting me. She had been looking for someone on LinkedIn to speak to about lead generation, and came across a video of mine in her feed. She looked at my profile, and all the recommendations from people I have worked with. She then spent a couple of hours going over all of my recent posts, and became convinced that I was the person she needed to speak to for help in generating more leads on LinkedIn.

Every week you will see tips from me about leveraging LinkedIn effectively. Every week I receive requests for interviews to speak at events or on podcasts to further share my expertise, and of course messages from people requesting conversations about how we could work together.

Using your community as a platform for problem solving is the fastest way to start creating the advocates you need to bring this process home (more about that in the next chapter).

Also, you can and should utilise other groups to share your expertise. LinkedIn allows you to be a member of up to one hundred groups. Find a select few that have a reasonable following and are likely to have a number of your ideal client avatars as members. Where you can, share your knowledge when the right questions are asked, and where appropriate you will get the opportunity to invite these people to join your community to access more direct assistance. The more you are seen as the problem solver in these groups, and on LinkedIn in general, the more trust you create.

Your problems

As I alluded to earlier, there are two problems I see regularly that are created by increased influence. The whole point of the exercise is to create more opportunities to attract new clients and increase your annual revenue. However, if these flaws exist in your next steps, a lot of your existing, and soon to be increasing, conversations will not hit the mark. You risk becoming very busy attempting to find time to have your sales conversations, and very busy writing proposals. At first that might seem like the best problem to have, and, granted, in some ways it would be.

This book is about the process of getting you to the point of receiving these types of messages on a regular basis, but the real game changer is what happens once you do. To be honest, this section, which is the next step after becoming an influencer, could be an entire book in itself. That's not possible, but I'd feel like I had led you to the promised land and left you high and dry if I didn't cover this in at least a small amount of detail.

There are two ways that you can enjoy a higher conversion rate.

Once you have completed the influencer framework and have become that go-to person, your conversations will always be about the problem you solve. Every week I get messages on LinkedIn like this one: *An associate of mine recommended you in a Neil Patel paid mastermind group as someone who is really keyed-in on LinkedIn. I've got 16,000 connections but I don't monetize it well. I'd love to connect and learn from you.*

Or like this one: *I've been following your content here on LinkedIn for a while and just saw your latest video (9-step formula on writing the ideal LinkedIn summary) and found it very interesting. I am keen to connect and understand how you can help me use LinkedIn more effectively.*

It's at this point that all the hard work could be undone very quickly and potentially tens of thousands, or even hundreds of thousands, of dollars lost.

My first suggestion is to make sure you have a booking scheduler that you can share with people to book in times to connect with you. I often see opportunities being lost that could so easily have been avoided through the use of this simple tool.

Let me share two scenarios using one of the above conversations.

Scenario #1: *Hi Jason, thanks for connecting and glad to hear you have found the videos, etc, useful. It would be my pleasure to touch base with you and discuss how we might be able to assist. When is a good time for you? Regards, Adam.*

This point is the beginning of an exhausting back-and-forward dialogue as I try to align Jason and my schedules to find a time to have a conversation. Most people check their LinkedIn accounts only once per day, twice if you're lucky, so by the time they have sent their message and you have seen it and responded, they will probably be gone for the day, as far as checking messages goes at least.

One of the shortcomings of the LinkedIn messaging system is the free messaging service. It's not an issue if you use Sales Navigator and understand how to track conversations with it, but the majority of people sending you a message will not have it, and may not be able to keep track of conversations even if they do.

The problem is that once someone reads your message there's no easy way for them to keep that message separate from the stream of incoming messages they receive afterwards, which means it's easily lost in the feed for both them and you. Out of sight out of mind, as the saying goes.

Often when we start working with new clients and looking at their recent activity, we see lost opportunities that have never resulted in a conversation.

The message simply gets lost, and it's too hard to align two busy people's schedules.

Scenario #2: *Hi Jason, thanks for connecting and glad to hear you have found the videos, etc, useful. It would be my pleasure to touch base with you and discuss how we might be able to assist. Just select a day and time that suits you here (add link to booking scheduler), anything showing open works for me, you can choose whether you prefer a phone chat or a zoom session, too. I look forward to connecting very soon. Regards, Adam.*

This scenario eliminates days of back-and-forward messaging trying to find a day and time to connect, and it also means that the conversation has moved off LinkedIn. If you don't hear back from your Jason within forty-eight hours you will simply follow up again with the link. The program I use for this is Schedule Once, but two others are Calendly and Acuity. Check them out and set one up as soon as you finish reading this chapter.

The second big time drain eventuates once your meeting is booked and you're set to outline how you're going to solve your potential new client's problem when you connect. If, like the majority of your competitors, you offer a service, you will probably spend a large part of your sales conversations explaining what it is. Wherever possible, it's far better to have a product that is your service. Having to quote individually on every opportunity, or having to explain what your service is and how it solves someone's problem is time consuming. Also, all your hard work could get you to this point and end in confusion, or your potential new client needs time to think about it, or, even worse, your potential new client decides to shop your quote around other service providers.

Granted, it's not always possible to productise a service, but wherever possible you should do this. In most cases when I have spoken with clients about this, and they believe they cannot productise, we've found ways that they can. Or at the very least we have created a range of products.

As an example, we have a DIY program, with Done With You and Done For You options. One hundred percent of the people we speak to fit into one of these three options, so the conversation is simply around which one will solve their problem best. The outcome is an efficient conversation, with almost no time spent on following up with time-consuming quotes or proposals.

In this scenario, the product information is always the same, as is the price, making it easy for someone who has already been through their journey of getting to know who you are, liking what you do, and having enough trust to reach out to you and make the decision to become a client.

Using a booking scheduler, and having products, will solve two big problems that you will face as a result of the increased interest you will create once you become highly influential.

Clarity Message

Annemarie Cross

Anne Marie is known as 'the podcasting queen'. She helps busy change makers go from invisible to influential through podcasting. She is the founder of 'Podcasting With Purpose', an agency dedicated to Done With You and Done For You podcast services.

What was the biggest challenge you were having with LinkedIn before doing the 12-Week Influencer Program?

As a podcast-production network, we have many podcast interviews that we continue to share on behalf of our clients and our guests. We were sharing these interviews via external links to each client's podcast episode, which meant that our content was not being seen. In fact, LinkedIn had us in LinkedIn jail, as Adam would call it.

How has your time spent on LinkedIn changed since completing the program?

I have refined my message into a miconiche, and now our overhauled profile and content is generating leads, enquiries and clients into our business pipeline. My content is now cutting through the noise and speaking to our ideal client, who is now engaging with me and messaging me privately for more information, which is ultimately our goal.

I have on-brand content going out consistently, which taps into text and video, both generating the likes and engagement I was unable to achieve prior. I also have a direct outreach process in place, which is generating conversations with our ideal customers and adding to our sales pipeline, something that was hit and miss previously.

Can you share one or two amazing benefits you have experienced since completing the program?

After overhauling my LinkedIn profile to speak directly to the issues my ideal client is struggling with, someone (who didn't know me) contacted me via phone after having just read it, saying, 'You are speaking to *me* and I just felt compelled to ring you.'

'So what do you do?' she asked me. To which I replied, 'You know how you read my introduction and felt as if I knew you, what you were struggling with, and you felt compelled to stop what you were doing to contact me?' 'Yes!' she responded. 'Well, that's *exactly* what I help my clients do, however with a podcast series.'

I've had similar conversations with people who have never met me before; however, after reading my content on LinkedIn and my profile, they are now in our pipeline for a Done-For-You podcast Series, our VIP offering, as well as our Done With You podcast platform.

This would not have happened were it not for the consistent, on-brand, microniche activity that I am regularly creating on LinkedIn.

How has this impacted you, either personally or as results for your business?

Prior to doing the influencer course, I had full intentions of no longer spending much time on LinkedIn due to the changes that had resulted in engagement plummeting and little traction. LinkedIn has now become *the* platform where our business is focusing our attention due to the quality of connections, engagement and business we are generating.

In fact, the majority of our high-end projects coming up in the next quarter (starting from $6000 and upwards) have been generated through LinkedIn.

Annemarie Cross

www.linkedin.com/in/annemariecross

www.podcastingwithpurpose.com

CHAPTER 13

Creating Advocates

And so we arrive at the last of our nine drivers of influencer. In the previous chapter I mentioned an important concept, which I'll quickly repeat here: you will only have achieved influencer status when other people say you have, not when *you* say you have.

Social media is awash with self-proclaimed experts, influencers, thought leaders, gurus and game changers. This is the fake-it-till-you-make-it crowd; their egos are not backed up by their results. True influencers don't need to proclaim these titles; instead, they are bestowed upon them by their communities. The titles are earned not claimed. Whether or not you add this status to your title is entirely up to you. More important is the way you influence some of your tribe to move from being members of your community or consumers of your content to becoming advocates.

Advocates are people who publicly support or recommend you. When enough of these people have made this move, the title of influencer has been bestowed. There is no magic number denoting that you have made it; you should view this very important concept as a work in progress. And there is one other very important thing to remember. The title can be yours simply by other people bestowing it on you; it can also disappear if they stop.

There are two very important ways in which your advocates bestow this title upon you, and you can easily control the flow of one of these. Let's start with the one you can control, and look at how you can go about doing that on a regular basis.

For a demonstration of this concept, scroll down to the section recommendations in my profile: www.linkedin.com/in/adamhoulahan. You will see many that refer specifically to programs we run, such as the 12-Week Influencer Challenge, and others from people who found enough value in the problem-solving content I regularly share that they were compelled to publicly state their beliefs.

LinkedIn Recommendations

An important part of your strategy as you move forward should be to regularly entice people to give you a LinkedIn recommendation. You can even do this retrospectively by reaching out to current or former clients and colleagues you have worked with and simply ask them if they would mind doing you this honour. As long as you are both first-degree connections on LinkedIn, anyone can supply you with an official LinkedIn recommendation.

A word of warning: don't engage in the practice of swapping recommendations. Nothing on your journey to becoming an influencer is about being artificial; in fact, it's quite the opposite. Being an influencer is simply a framework you can follow to achieve your desired outcomes.

Many people who reach out to you on LinkedIn will not know you, and will never have worked with you as a colleague or client. They might offer to give you a recommendation provided you return the favour. Be aware that the recommendations you receive, and the ones you give, appear on your profile with links to the other people's profiles, showing the dates the recommendations were given. Nothing looks more contrived than every person who has given you a recommendation receiving one from you in return.

This is equally relevant with regard to people you do know and have worked with, so avoid asking your colleagues and clients to swap recommendations with you. Of course, there will be times when you will be quite justified in giving a recommendation to someone who has given you one, but make sure the recommendations are not done in close time proximity to each other.

Genuine recommendations

Here is my very simple 4-point guide to receiving genuine recommendations:

1. Go through your cell-phone contacts or client files and make a list of people you have worked with as a colleague, or who were or are clients. From this list create a shortlist of people you believe you know well enough to have a conversation with about supplying you with a recommendation. They should be people you have had, or currently have, good rapport with, or whom you know have achieved exceptional outcomes through your services.

2. Pick up the phone and give three of these people a call. Add a reminder in your schedule to do this every week going forward until you run

out of people to talk to. I guarantee that if you select the right people, your strike rate will be exceptional if you have the a conversation along the following lines first:

Hey, Kylie, Adam Houlahan here [polite conversation about family, work, weather, etc]. *Kylie, there was actually a specific reason I wanted to reach out to you today. I'm putting some real effort into my LinkedIn profile at the moment and as part of that I need to get some recommendations. However, I want to be really authentic and make sure they are from people I have worked with in the past. I know you got great value from the work we did together. Would you be open to writing a few sentences in your own words about how I helped you?*

3. Let your new recommender know that you will send them a link on LinkedIn that will enable them to do this very easily. Almost everyone you have this conversation with will agree to do this for you, but most will be busy people just like you. Despite their good intentions, work and life could get in the way, so making it as easy as possible for them will improve the results dramatically.

    LinkedIn allows you to request recommendations, which you can do in three easy steps. First, on LinkedIn find the person you had your conversation with. Below their professional headline you will see the More tab. Click on this, and then click on Request a Recommendation.

    You now have the option to select both your relationship and your position at the time you and this other person worked together. You will see many options that should cover every scenario, so simply choose the most appropriate.

You can now add a short message to be sent with your request. By default, it will say something bland like, *Hi Kylie, can you write me a recommendation?* Delete the default message and create a more personal note referencing your recent phone conversation and then hit send.

Follow up by sending Kylie a text message or email to say that you have sent her your recommendation request, and ask her to check her messages on LinkedIn. Reiterate your appreciation for doing this for you.

4. As you move forward, you will find yourself working with more and more people, and you should still go through the above process with each one at the appropriate time. This shouldn't be at the beginning of your working relationship, and when you do it will depend on how your services work. If you have been given a set task with a defined outcome or a result that you deliver, the appropriate time would be when you have delivered on your promise. If you work with people over a long timeframe or an ongoing capacity, the right time will be up to your best judgement, but ideally it should be after a few months of working together, or when they have achieved a tangible outcome.

Content comments

As mentioned earlier, there is another equally important way for your advocates to bestow the honour of influencer on you; however, it's less controllable than recommendations. This is via the comments on your content on LinkedIn and most importantly where your advocates choose to create their own content about you.

At first glance, it might seem that this is easily managed by simply asking people to do it in the same way that you ask for recommendations. But the type of content I'm referring to is not something you could easily ask someone for, at least not in my opinion. Instead, your advocates will create and share this type of content about you as a direct result of you focusing on providing great advice and being the problem solver.

Here are some examples of comments from my own clients:

- *I know and highly recommend Adam Houlahan as a LinkedIn expert trainer! I also just finished his latest book recently and recommend that as well. #business #linkedin*
- *Thanks for trying your best to work with very little #headshots #business #training #communication #fundraising #innovative #lifelonglearning #mentors Adam Houlahan #littlesteps*
- *Adam Houlahan and Michael (Mike) Clark sharing some sage LinkedIn wisdom here at WOTSO on the Gold Coast.*
- *Adam Houlahan is a social media expert who has had a fascinating career journey. As part of my #14InspiringLeaders podcast series, I've chosen Adam's interview out of 150 episodes to share as it'll provide inspiration to anyone considering entrepreneurship. Listen to his story, from his early childhood aspirations to join the Air Force, to creating a lifestyle business, becoming a waterski instructor to owning a chain of waterski businesses ... but how did he become the author of Secret*

Sauce and the sought after social media strategist and expert he is today? You'll enjoy our conversation here: #podcasting #entrepreneurship #JaneCareerCoach #AdamHoulahan

- *How do you take time to enjoy life & learn? We work so hard & must recharge our batteries I ✈ over 10 hours to Budapest Hungary. When I have quiet time on the plane or early in the mornings is when I recharge and think about my goals & my life direction. Adam Houlahan's Play Book is my learning tool on the trip. I am joining 50 Entrepreneurs' Organization members & their spouses on a Avalon River Boat Cruise on the Danube River Avalon Waterways River Cruises #linkedingoals #enjoyment #Avalon #cruises*

Sharing of your content and commenting on your content will come from you: from your constant focus on creating exceptional content week after week (see chapter 10), and from you engaging on their comments (see chapter 9).

This is not something that you need to control; the more organically and naturally it occurs the more power it will possess. Rest assured that this is where true influence lies. And here I'll repeat that little phrase for the last time: you will only have achieved influencer status when other people say you have, not when *you* do.

If I were to put a label on the process that is the 9-step guide to becoming highly influential in any industry, it would be *authority marking*. Do your online searches and you will find no shortage of articles about this, and thought leadership or similar. It's mostly good content, and I not only agree with the concepts of authority marketing, but I have also lived by the principals for quite a few years now.

Is it the only form of marketing you should pursue? No, it isn't. Will it be the right methodology for every person who reads it? No, it will not. Is influence easy to obtain? I believe it is as easy as you choose to make it.

I've attempted to make this book similar to my earlier book, *The LinkedIn Playbook*; that is, I have written it as a playbook. It's designed to be a reference guide that you work your way through methodically, step by step, and come back to regularly over time. In this way you will get a sense of what you have achieved as you implement each step and cross it off your to-do list.

I have received many messages from people all over the world who have implemented the strategies from *The LinkedIn Playbook* and gone on to generate millions of dollars of combined revenue by following the outlined steps and adapting them to their individual circumstances. It is my hope that *Influencer* will sit on your desk, or within easy reach on your bookshelf, and that you'll refer to it regularly. Better still, keep both books together. *Influencer* does not supersede *The LinkedIn Playbook*, or in any way make the earlier book redundant. It is a valuable resource in itself and should be considered an extension of the principals and action steps outlined in *The LinkedIn Playbook*.

Influencer is complete in its own right, but the power of combining both books will only deepen your experience and knowledge of leveraging this incredible platform that is LinkedIn.

MY GIFTS TO YOU

I do hope you enjoyed reading this book as much as I enjoyed the process of writing it, and not just the process of writing it, but also the thousands of hours of research, and the trial and error that went into validating the processes I have outlined before even putting pen to paper. More importantly, it's my hope that you will undertake your own journey to influence and reap the rewards I know await you. Please do share your journey with me; nothing excites me more than receiving those messages via email or LinkedIn.

You will find more resources that support this book on my website: www.adamhoulahan.com.

Gift #1: A free copy of The LinkedIn Playbook

You can access a free download of my last book *The LinkedIn Playbook* from our private group: LinkedIn2Success www.facebook.com/groups/LinkedIn2Success. This is our Facebook community, where smart entrepreneurs learn to get more leads and effective ways to scale using LinkedIn, so please do request to join today. It's also where we will keep you up to date on all the latest things happening on LinkedIn.

Gift #2: Discounted access to the 12-Week Influencer Program

By purchasing this book you have taken the first step in your journey to influence through our 12-Week Influencer Program. The program gives you the opportunity to take the learning you have attained and accelerate your ability to create influence to even greater heights. To access the discount code, send an email with the subject line 'influencer discount': clientdelight@webtrafficthatworks.com.

Gift #3: The gift of giving

I consider it one of my greatest privileges to support so many charities through each of my books and the programs we have developed for entrepreneurs around the world. I'm proud to say that we have created over one million impacts, or 'smiles', as we like to call them.

By purchasing a copy of this book, you have helped provide an e-learning facility for a rural village. In fact, as a result of your purchase eleven children gained access to the best learning environment available by introducing them to the latest technology for effective learning.

To meet the demands of today's global economy, it's crucial that all children receive quality education that equips them with 21st-century skills. Doing this together with you is a small yet important step in improving the lives of children who, without our support, would miss out on vital education.

I believe that real and meaningful change comes through the world's entrepreneurs; people just like you. My purpose is to help you create a powerful online presence that grows and accelerates your global footprint, so that together we can make a huge impact. You can access further information about the causes we support here: www.adamhoulahan.com/impact.

If you have read any of my previous books or been to my website, you know that I love quotes. Once again, I would like to leave you with one of my favourites, by Roy T Bennett: 'One of the best ways to influence people is to make them feel important. Most people enjoy those rare moments when others make them feel important. It is one of the deepest human desires.'